3 Speak NOW

COMMUNICATE with CONFIDENCE

Teacher's BOOK

Jack C. Richards
David Bohlke
Carmella Lieske

OXFORD
UNIVERSITY PRESS

3 Speak NOW
Level Guide

Expand the *Speak Now* **Student Book lessons** with activities from the Multi-Skill Bonus Pack, available on iTools. This Level Guide provides you with a map of the course's various resources, allowing you to build a rich and comprehensive syllabus. Through targeted expansion activities, students gain confidence in English across every skill area.

Multi-Skill Bonus Pack Worksheets

VOCABULARY	READING AND WRITING	GRAMMAR Power Point™ Support	LEARNING OUTCOMES Now I can...
Family	English Practice Pals	**A:** Uses of need	...talk about people.
Personality types	Student Union President Elections	**B:** Expressions of quantity	...describe family relationships.
Describing people	Family drama	**C:** Using pretty	
Values	My Hero		
At a hotel	Where to stay		...address problems on vacation.
Rules	New way to stay	**A:** Noun clauses	
Problems and complaints	Dew Drop Inn		...accept or decline help.
Customer service	Tourism service careers		
Around town	Visit to Rio		...make appointments and point out mistakes.
Apologies	The Secret Shopper Scoop	**A:** Relative clauses	
Appointments	Tips for making medical appointments		...make recommendations.
Problems	Teen Time		
Childhood	Do-overs		...talk about the past.
Reactions	Best Books	**A:** Past tenses	
Headlines	Weird News Stories		...state when things happened.
Events	What makes something news?		

3 Speak NOW
Level Guide

Multi-Skill Bonus Pack Worksheets

VOCABULARY	READING AND WRITING	GRAMMAR Power Point™ Support	LEARNING OUTCOMES *Now I can...*
Friends	Types of friends		
Friendship traits	Welcome to English 101!	**A:** Conditionals	...discuss what's important to friends.
Making friends	Miss you		...offer solutions to a problem.
Resolutions	Cyber Billy		
Qualifications	Final candidates for Regional Sales Manager		
Advertisements	Advertising across cultures	**A:** Reported speech	...talk about job qualifications.
Business trends	Trendspotting	**B:** Reporting verbs	...describe trends.
Business reviews	Can a bookstore succeed?		
Customs	Study Abroad Culture Guide	**A:** Word order of adjectives	...compare cultural differences.
Proverbs	Proverbs about appearance		
Superstitions	Wedding plans	**B:** Anything, Anyone, Nothing, No one	...ask about and describe consequences.
News	Who made the Nazca Lines?		
The future	What may happen		
Science	The Great Pacific Garbage Patch	**A:** Habitual present vs. Future time	...predict the future.
Chores	Weekend plans	**B:** Future time continued	...discuss goals and wishes.
Goals	Graduation and beyond		

Teacher's Book Contents

Teacher's Book Contents (continued)

The *Speak Now Testing Program CD-ROM* contains the following:

Spoken Interview Placement Test

Scoring Rubric and Testing Instructions

Quizzes

Quiz 1	Quiz 5	Quizzes Answer Key
Quiz 2	Quiz 6	Quizzes Audio Script
Quiz 3	Quiz 7	
Quiz 4	Quiz 8	

Speaking Assessment: General

Presentation Topics	Presentation Feedback Form
Interview Questions	Presentation Tips
Role-Plays	

Midterm Exam: Written; Speaking Assessment in the form of Standardized Tests

Midterm Written Exam	Midterm Exam IELTS™ style
Midterm Exam TOEFL® style	Midterm Written Exam Answer Key
Midterm Exam TOEIC® style	Midterm Exam Audio Scripts

Final Exam: Written; Speaking Assessment in the form of Standardized Tests

Final Written Exam	Final Exam IELTS™ style
Final Exam TOEFL® style	Final Exam Answer Key
Final Exam TOEIC® style	Final Exam Audio Scripts

Additional Teacher Resources

Speak Now 3 Video Scripts	Speak Now 3 Class Audio Script

TOEFL® and TOEIC® are registered trademarks of Educational Testing Services (ETS). This publication is not endorsed or approved by ETS.

How to teach a *Speak Now* lesson

Each lesson has five parts—Vocabulary, Conversation, Language Booster, Listening or Pronunciation, and Speak with Confidence.

Lesson Introduction

- Read the lesson title as students follow along. When applicable, have students answer the question.
- Point out the functions they will be studying and explain them or reword them when necessary.

1 Vocabulary

The purpose of this section is to get students thinking about the topic, activate their background knowledge, and introduce them to vocabulary that they will use during the lesson. To prepare the students to use the vocabulary, preteach it. When the vocabulary is unfamiliar to your students, present it through visual aids (for example, photos), actions and gestures, and rephrasing or English definitions.

- If necessary, have students use an English Learners' dictionary, perhaps before coming to class, to better understand not only the meanings but also how to use the words.
- Avoid giving students definitions in their first language. Although doing so may initially save time, students do not acquire the language as thoroughly and will rely on their first language rather than developing their English ability. In addition, nuances in languages often vary, creating additional complications as students continue to use the language.
- When you have time, further reinforce the vocabulary with personalization (for example, using the vocabulary in true sentences about themselves).

2 Conversation

There are two types of lesson patterns for the Conversation section. Some of the lessons follow the "Conversation with Additions" model and others follow the "Conversation with Expansions" model. Teaching procedures for each lesson pattern are outlined below. Both conversations follow the same procedure for Part A.

Conversation with Additions

A

- This section helps students become comfortable with the topic and provides a model conversation that uses the functional language from the Language Booster section.
- Read the questions aloud. Ask students to guess the answers by looking at the photos or illustrations. Ask students questions about details in the art.
- Play the audio and select students to answer the questions. If necessary, play the audio again.
- Make sure students understand the answers to the questions by asking concept questions or reforming the question to check understanding.

B

By practicing the conversation, students become more aware of functional language and more comfortable with language in "chunks". This prepares them for the Language Booster section and will also help them notice the changes in Part C.

C

- Tell students that they will listen to the conversation again, but three sentences are on the audio program which are not printed in the book. Explain that they should write the sentences they hear in the correct places.
- Play the audio. Check answers. If necessary, have students compare answers in pairs, play the audio again, and then check answers as a class.
- After checking answers, play the audio again so students can focus on the pronunciation and intonation. Have students pay attention to the words they did not understand before.
- Have students practice the conversation at least two times, once for each role.

2 Conversation with Expansions

A

- Follow the same procedure as Conversation with Additions, Part A.

B

- Practice the conversation in Part A.
- Have students read the sentences below the conversation. They should place the expansion

sentences in the conversation by writing the number of the sentence in the correct place within the conversation.

- Check answers as a class. Provide any language support that may be needed (for example, pronunciation of the boxed text).
- Encourage students to read the new conversation aloud. Students should practice both roles and look at each other rather than their books.
- Students who finish the activities quickly can practice the conversation again with their own substitutions.

3 Language Booster

A

This activity provides students with examples of the target language. In almost every lesson, the language includes both questions and responses. You may want to have students practice the language (i.e., take turns asking and answering the questions) before going on to Part B.

B

- This activity allows students to gain confidence as they use the language in short exchanges. This will provide them with the skills to make longer dialogues later in the lesson.
- In mixed ability classes, have students with lower English levels make some notes or sentence starters before they do the activity. These aids will help them to successfully complete the activity and further increase their confidence.
- After students have finished the activity, you may want to randomly choose a few pairs and have them role-play the conversations at the front of the classroom.
- After completing Part B, if students aren't confident with the language, have them continue practicing until they have more confidence. They can even make small substitutions to do this.

4 Listening

- The purpose of this activity is to help students focus on main ideas and details in the listening. Students may listen as many times as needed.
- After students have listened several times, you may want to stop the audio at key points so students can more easily complete the task.
- The Listening often concludes with a pair work activity that allows students to personalize what they have heard.

4 Pronunciation

- This section begins by helping students focus on pronunciation or intonation through listening. Students then practice the Pronunciation point. Students may tend to focus on the content and quickly forget to pay attention to their pronunciation and intonation. If this happens, briefly stop the class to remind students that they are practicing both content and pronunciation and then have them continue their practice.
- Play the audio, repeating as necessary.
- Ask students obvious questions to make sure they understand the point. For example, if you are teaching syllables, say some words and ask students how many syllables are in them.
- To give students more practice with the language, include all class (choral), group, individual, and substitution drills. This additional practice will give students more confidence and reinforce the pronunciation before they return to focusing more on content.

Speak with Confidence

- This activity allows students to use the target language as they accomplish defined tasks.
- Part A helps students prepare for their interactions in Part B.

Lesson Expansion

Vocabulary Worksheets

- After you have completed the Language Booster activities you can use the Vocabulary Worksheets for supplementary practice.
- The worksheets provide additional opportunities for students to practice the vocabulary and language studied in each lesson.
- Take advantage of the opportunities for additional speaking by having students compare their answers in class. Example conversations are often provided on the worksheets.

Reading and Writing Worksheets

- Reading and Writing Worksheets may be found on the iTools CD-ROM or on Oxford Learn, Oxford's Learning Management System. Access Oxford Learn with the code provided in the back of this book.

How to teach a review unit

Each review unit has two sections, *English in Action*, which includes a video, and *Speak Now*, which gives students the opportunity to role-play situations and at the same time review the language of the previous four lessons.

English in Action

- Video is a great way to introduce longer dialogues to students. The video makes the long dialogues less threatening and helps students understand language that otherwise might seem overwhelming to them.
- Video is exciting and different for students, and as a result, it can be both stimulating and motivating.
- Using video is similar to teaching a listening or reading activity—there is a pre-video activity. On the *English in Action* page, this is called **Preview**. After this, there are one or more "while you watch" activities. On the *English in Action* page, this is **Understand**. These activities include comprehension questions to check students' understanding. These activities usually require two or more viewings. Finally, there is a post-video activity. On the *English in Action* page, this is **Discuss**.
- Before class, make certain your classroom's Internet connection, computer, and projector are working properly.

1 Preview

- Students are asked to look at one or more photos from the video that they will watch in Part 2. With a partner, they talk about what they see. They also often make predictions.
- When possible, use this opportunity to have students talk about what they see in more detail. For example, the Preview for Lessons 9-12 asks students to talk about exciting things to do in New York. You could have them brainstorm other activities to do in a new city, other than the ones the photos suggest.

2 Understand

During Part 2, students watch a video that recycles content, vocabulary, and language they have studied during the last four lessons. This allows students to see the material used in real-world situations and apply their learning more broadly.

A

- Explain what students must do (for example, they should number photos in Part 1 or listen and decide if their predications were correct).
- Play the video. Have students answer the questions in pairs or as a class.

B

- Part B asks students to listen for more details.
- Play the video and then have students answer the questions in pairs or as a class.
- Play the video again, as necessary, stopping to explain where an answer was within the dialogue.

3 Discuss

- The Discuss activity allows students to personalize what they saw.
- After students finish their discussions, have them do the **Confidence Booster** at the back of their books. This provides further reinforcement and review of the four units.

Speak Now

- In pairs, have students role-play each situation.
- After they have finished practicing, have some pairs role-play for the class.
- Remind students to assess their own abilities for each lesson. For any Lessons that they check *I need more practice*, encourage them to review the Language Boosters. (Page numbers are provided on the Speak Now review pages.)
- For a formal assessment, a Testing Program CD-ROM accompanies this book.

Review Unit Expansion
Video Worksheets

- Video Worksheets with a cloze/gap fill activity may be found on the iTools CD-ROM or on Oxford Learn. Access Oxford Learn with the code provided in the back of this book.
- These worksheets provide additional listening practice for the *English in Action* video.

Grammar Support

- Grammar PowerPoint™ presentations and Grammar Worksheets may be found on the iTools CD-ROM or Oxford Learn.

Speak Now Testing Program Overview

The *Speak Now* series helps learners Communicate with Confidence by using language accurately, fluently, and appropriately. The *Speak Now Testing Program,* found on the CD-ROM in the back of this book, allows teachers to perform a wide range of assessments—many in the style of popular standardized exams.

Speak Now's written and oral assessment tools can be customized to fit the needs of a range of program types and learning goals.

The Testing Program offers two main sets of tools:

1. **10 paper-based tests: 8 quizzes, 1 midterm exam, and 1 final exam** with listening that measure comprehension of the vocabulary and functional language of *Speak Now*

2. a range of different types of questions, prompts, and topics for **speaking assessment**.

Teachers may choose to use any one or more of these materials alone or in different combinations. The **Scoring Guidelines** can be found on the *Speak Now Testing Program CD-ROM*.

Written Tests with Listening

There is a quiz for each 4-lesson unit of *Speak Now*. The **quizzes** are designed to be used after students have completed each group of four lessons and Speak Now review section in the Student Book. The quizzes have 10 items each. There is an audio track for the listening items in each quiz on the *Speak Now Testing Program CD-ROM*.

There is also a written **midterm exam** and a written **final exam**. These are designed to measure comprehension of the target language after students have completed Lesson 16 and Lesson 32 of the book, respectively. The midterm and final exams have 20 items each. There is an audio track for the listening items in each exam on the *Speak Now Testing Program CD-ROM*.

All answer keys and audio scripts are on the *Speak Now Testing Program CD-ROM*.

Speaking Assessment: General

The *Speak Now Testing Program* offers options for speaking assessment:

- **Interview questions** (a list of teacher-led interview questions)
- **Role-play cards** (cards for students to role-play situations in pairs)
- **Presentation topics** (lists of ideas for students to prepare and deliver short oral presentations related to the unit topics)

The *Speak Now Testing Program* features one set of the three speaking-assessment options profiled above for each unit or set of four lessons. Any or all of the speaking assessments can easily be used after students have completed a unit of work. To use these materials for midterm or end-of-term speaking assessment, simply choose from this list of materials, based on the units covered in the class.

Speaking Assessment: Standardized-testing Focus

The *Speak Now Testing Program CD-ROM* also offers speaking assessment in the style of popular standardized tests of English as a foreign language. For each **midterm exam** and **final exam**, you'll find:

- **TOEFL®-style speaking tasks**
- **TOEIC®-style speaking tasks**
- **IELTS™-style speaking tasks**

The goal of these standardized-testing tasks is to prepare students for the kinds of questions they would be asked on exams such as the TOEFL®, TOEIC®, or IELTS™ tests. As these materials are preparatory in nature, the rubrics do not reflect the type of scoring or grading that a test-taker would receive in a standardized testing situation.

TOEFL® and TOEIC® are registered trademarks of Educational Testing Services (ETS). This publication is not endorsed or approved by ETS.

Lesson 1 I'm an only child.

Page 2

1 Vocabulary

A

Answers			
single	engaged	middle child	fiancée

Optional Activity

Teach students other vocabulary related to family, for example:

An extended family	The family unit that includes grandparents, parents, siblings, aunts, uncles, and cousins.
A nuclear family	The family unit that includes the father, mother, and children.
The baby of the family	The youngest child.
In-law	Family members through marriage. For example, my sister's husband is my brother-in-law. We only use in-law with brother, sister, mother, and father. For other relationships, we do not differentiate relatives through marriage and birth (for example, we don't say aunt-in-law).

2 Conversation

A

[CD 1, Track 2]

Answers
Isabel is going to a birthday party for her grandmother's 80th birthday. Isabel has five siblings.

- Explain that when we count family members, we include ourselves. As a result, Isabel has eight people in her family—her mom, dad, three older brothers, two sisters, and herself.
- Tell students that we don't include ourselves in the number of brothers and sisters we have (i.e., the number of siblings).

Optional Activity

How to count family members may be unusual for students who, when speaking in their first language, include themselves in the number of siblings. Have students practice the following conversation several times.

Example conversation

A: How many brothers and sisters do you have?

B: One—my sister.

A: And how many people are in your family?

B: Three—my mom, my sister and me.

C

[CD 1, Track 3]

Answers
Additional sentences underlined. John: Are you waiting for someone? <u>Where are you going?</u> Isabel: Yeah, my brother. … It's her 80th birthday. <u>Everyone will be there.</u> John: Wow! You have a big family. <u>I didn't know that.</u>

Page 3

4 Pronunciation

A

[CD 1, Track 4]

Remind students that we never stress words that don't contribute to actual meaning (for example, an).

B

[CD 1, Track 5]

Answers	
1. only child	**2.** Roger, baby, family

5 Speak with Confidence

A

Example conversation

A: Would you like more siblings?

B: No, I wouldn't.

A: Who are your parents' siblings?

B: My Aunt Mariko and my Uncle Noriyuki.

A: What kind of family would you like to have someday?

B: I want a big family, with three or four children.

Lesson 2 She's a born leader.

Page 4
1 Vocabulary

A

Answers	
1. f	5. h
2. g	6. e
3. b	7. c
4. a	8. d

2 Conversation

A

[CD 1, Track 6]

Answers
Andy and Kit think Amy would be the best choice for student union president because she's a born leader and an optimist. Richard is a lot of fun, but he's kind of a know-it-all.

B

Answers
Andy: Who would be a good person for student union president? 2 Andy: And she's an optimist. I like that. 3 Kit: There's also that new student—Richard. What do you think of him? 4 Andy: Well, he's a lot of fun, but he's kind of a know-it-all. 1

Page 5
3 Language Booster

A

• Point out that we can use both *who* and *that* to connect a clause (i.e., a phrase) with the person it describes.

• Explain that rephrasing is an important skill that allows the listener to understand a word that he/she may not know. Have students find the examples of this (*a born leader* is explained as *someone who leads naturally* and *an optimist* is explained *as always positive*.)

B

Encourage students to also use rephrasing like that in Part A.

Example conversation

A: Jie is a pessimist. She's always negative.

B: Yeah, but she's also a problem solver. Marco is a born leader.

A: And he's also a role model.

4 Listening

A

[CD 1, Track 7]

Answers	
Maya	role model
Roberto	optimist
Bernadette	problem solver
Young-Ho	loner

B

[CD 1, Track 7]

Answers	
Answers will vary. Sample answer.	
Maya	I volunteer at a school in an underdeveloped neighborhood. I try to set a good example and encourage the students to study.
Roberto	I try to focus on the positive. I think things will work out for the best.
Bernadette	I'm the type of person who tries to fix things. It always feels satisfying when I can solve something.
Young-Ho	I prefer to do things on my own. I like people, but I also really enjoy my own time.

5 Speak with Confidence

A

Answers
Answers will vary. Sample answer.

	Yes	No		Yes	No
1.		✓	4.		✓
2.		✓	5.	✓	
3.	✓		6.	✓	

B

Example conversation

A: You said yes three times, so you're sometimes a leader and sometimes a follower.

B: That's true. You have five points, so you're definitely a leader.

Lesson 3 We're both reliable.

Page 6
1 Vocabulary

A

> **Answers**
>
> **Answers will vary.** Sample answer.
> P considerate   P flexible   P reliable   P mature
> P forgiving   N moody   P responsible
> N immature

Optional Activity

Have students brainstorm or teach other characteristics to describe people, having them decide if they are positive or negative. Examples include:

Positive: kind, open-minded, patient, sociable

Negative: judgmental, close-minded, temperamental

2 Conversation

A
[CD 1, Track 8]

> **Answers**
>
> Keisha and Kelly are both reliable.
> Keisha is more reliable than Kelly. Kelly is more flexible and more forgiving.

C
[CD 1, Track 9]

> **Answers**
>
> Additional sentences underlined.
> Sara: How similar are you and Kelly? <u>Or are you really different?</u>
> Keisha: She's more flexible than me. <u>She's a lot more flexible.</u>
> Keisha: She's the type of person who just goes with things…She lives by the motto, *"Forgive and forget."* <u>I forgive, but I never forget!</u>

Page 7
3 Language Booster

B

Example conversation

A: I'm a considerate person, and I'm not a judgmental person.

B: Me, too. I'm also very mature for my age.

4 Pronunciation

A
[CD 1, Track 10]

> **Answers**
>
> 1. **flex**ible   2. re**spon**sible
>   flexi**bil**ity   responsi**bil**ity

- Have students identify the number of syllables in each word, providing the answer if necessary (flexible 3, flexibility 5, responsible 4, responsibility 6). If students are having problems with this, break the words up into syllables, saying each one separately.
- Point out that two syllables are added when *ity* is added to the word. If necessary, remind students that *ity* is called a suffix.
- Point out that the stress changes when *ity* is added to the root (or base) word.
- Tell students that most suffixes don't change the stress, but that when *ity* is added, the syllable just before the suffix is stressed.

B
[CD 1, Track 11]

> **Answers**
>
> 1. ma**ture** / ma**tur**ity   4. re**li**able / relia**bil**ity
> 2. **gen**erous /   5. for**giv**ing /
>   gene**ros**ity   for**give**ness
> 3. sin**cere** / sin**cer**ity   6. **mood**y / moodiness

5 Speak with Confidence

B

Example conversation

A: I'm most similar to Massimo. We almost had the same answers!

Lesson 4 As I was saying…

1 Vocabulary

A

> **Answers**
>
> **Answers will vary.** Sample answer.
> Students should circle three values, for example:
> respect   honesty   loyalty

Optional Activity

Have students give an example that represents each value. For example, when you remain friends with someone in good and bad times, you show loyalty.

2 Conversation

A
[CD 1, Track 12]

> **Answers**
>
> Megan didn't keep the change the salesclerk gave her because that wouldn't be honest.
> The salesclerk gave Megan a special discount.

Optional Activity

Have students get into groups and talk about any experiences as a cashier. Encourage them to talk about what happens (i.e., the company policy) if there is a mistake in the amount of money in the cash register.

B

> **Answers**
>
> Megan: Hey, Derek. It's me. You'll never guess what happened. 2
> Megan: No, of course not. That wouldn't be honest. I gave it back. 4
> Megan: She was…She was so grateful that she offered me a special discount. 1
> Derek: She gave you a discount? 3

3 Language Booster

A

- Point out that the interruption always starts with an expression including *sorry* or *excuse me*. Tell students this shows the other person that the speaker realizes he/she is interrupting.
- Explain that by asking if it's OK to interrupt, the speaker gives the listener the option of refusing.

B

Remind students that it's rude to interrupt people, so although they are practicing, they should not overuse this skill.

4 Listening

A
[CD 1, Track 13]

> **Answers**
>
> 1. sacrificing   3. sympathy
> 2. respect   4. kindness

B
[CD 1, Track 13]

> **Answers**
>
> Her friends interrupt twice.
> First, the woman interrupts with, "Sorry to interrupt, Rachel, but why was the story important to you?"
> Later, the man interrupts by asking, "Can I ask a question? How can friendship not be important?"

Optional Activity

Have students listen again and write down what the friends said to interrupt. (Answers above.)

5 Speak with Confidence

A

> **Answers**
>
> **Answers will vary.** Sample answer.
> I learned honesty by seeing other people be honest when I was young.
> I learned honesty from my mother.
> This value is still especially important to me today.
> One way to teach this value is to let someone feel what it is like when someone isn't honest.

Lessons 1 to 4 Review

English in Action

Page 10

1 Preview

Answers
Answers will vary. Sample answer. No, Jill doesn't pack light. I pack like Jill when I travel. I bring too many things like clothes, shoes, and books.

2 Practice

Answers
1. F (Maria, Eric, Tom and Jill are going to go to New York.) 2. T 3. T 4. T 5. F (Eric's brother is the oldest child in Eric's family.) 6. F (Eric's brother is Tom's role model.) 7. F (Jill is going away for two days.)

B

Students should correct the false sentences.
Answers above.

Optional Questions

Is Jill often late? (Yes, she is. Eric said that Jill always says she's on her way, which is an excuse that is used when running late.)

How are they going to New York? (They are going by bus.)

What is Eric's brother like? (He's a people person. He's sociable and has a lot of friends. He's also a problem solver.)

3 Discuss

You might want to have students give reasons for their answers to the questions in 2 and 3.

Example conversation

A: Do you live near your family?

B: Yeah. How about you?

C: No. So, how would you describe Jill?

D: Well, it seems like she's late a lot, so I think she doesn't respect other people's time.

B: Yeah. Have you traveled anywhere recently? Where did you go? Did you travel with a friend?

A: I went to Hawaii last year. My family and I went for summer vacation.

Speak Now

Page 11

Provide an example of each conversation when necessary.

If many students need more practice with a particular unit, you might want to review it in class.

1 *Example conversation*

A: Do you have a large family?

B: Not really. I have a brother and just my mom and dad. My mom is the optimist. She's always positive. And my dad is a problem solver. No matter what the problem is, he can find a solution!

2 *Example conversation*

A: What is Gabrielle like?

B: She's a born leader. She's someone people naturally follow.

A: Is she a know-it-all? No one likes a know-it-all.

B: No, she's not. She's confident, but she listens to others. I think she'd be a good class representative.

3 *Example conversation*

A: My brother and I are both considerate.

B: Are you both flexible?

A: I try to be, but my brother is more flexible. But I'm more responsible. Sometimes my brother doesn't do the things he needs to do. It really frustrates my mom.

4 *Example conversation*

A: One person I admire is our teacher.

B: Sorry, but can I interrupt for a second? Why did you choose this topic instead of the other one?

A: Because I think I can talk about it for two minutes. Anyway, as I was saying, one person I admire is…

Lesson 5 I'd like to check in.

Optional Activity

Before students open their books, ask them about their travel experiences (for example, Have you ever been to another country? Do you like to travel?). Then have students name some popular reasons for traveling (for example, to sightsee, to try new food, to meet people).

Page 12
1 Vocabulary

A

> **Answers**
>
> **Answers will vary.** Sample answer. Students' additional answers are in bold.
> Places to stay: dorm, youth hostel, hotel, motel, campground, **bed and breakfast**
> Facilities: business center, pool, **gym**
> Types of rooms: dorm, single, double, triple, **non-smoking**

2 Conversation

A
[CD 1, Track 14]

> **Answers**
>
> Mira gives the clerk her passport and a credit card.
> Mira is staying for four nights.

Optional Question

What is the date of the conversation? (Mira is staying for four nights and checking out on the 16th, so it's the 12th.)

C
[CD 1, Track 15]

> **Answers**
>
> Additional sentences underlined.
> Mira: Hello...My name's Mira Abboud. <u>I have a reservation.</u>
> Mira: Sure. <u>Here is my card.</u>
> Mira: I don't think so. Thank you. <u>You've been very helpful.</u>

Page 13
4 Pronunciation

A
[CD 1, Track 16]

> **Answers**
>
> The following sounds should be blended together instead of saying the two words distinctly.
> **1.** ha**vea**   **2.** fi**llin**

Explain that students cannot just look at the spelling of the words to determine when to link sounds. Remind them that some vowels have consonant sounds. For example, *one* begins with the /w/ sound, so in the following question, *is* and *one* are not blended.

Is one queen size bed OK?

B

If students are having problems linking the sounds, have them first practice blending only the two words. Then have them add one or two words to the blend, and continue to add words until they are saying the complete sentences and questions with the linked sounds.

5 Speak with Confidence

Before students start, remind them that the Guest most provide all of the information necessary to check in (for example, how many nights, what type of room).

Example conversation

Hotel clerk:	Hello. Can I help you?
Guest:	I'd like to check in.
Hotel clerk:	Certainly. Do you have a reservation?
Guest:	Yes, I do. My name's Natasha Riviera. I'm staying for two nights in a double room.
Hotel clerk:	Ah yes. Here's your name. Can I see your I.D.?
Guest:	Of course. Here you go.
Hotel clerk:	Thank you. And could you fill in this registration card?
Guest:	Yes, of course.
Hotel clerk:	Is there anything more I can do for you?
Guest:	No, thank you.

Lesson 6 Here are some rules.

Optional Activity

Before students open their books, have them talk about places where there are rules (for example, at school, on the road for driving, at a job). Have them talk about why we need rules, providing reasons when possible. (For example, we need rules because some people aren't considerate. They don't think about other people, so we have to tell them what they should or shouldn't do.)

Page 14

1 Vocabulary

A

Answers
Answers will vary. Sample answer.
B **1.** Leave the key at the front desk.
Y **2.** No noise after midnight.
H **3.** Shower before entering the pool.
Y **4.** Kitchen for guests only.
Y **5.** Shared bathrooms on each floor.
H **6.** Health club hours: 10 a.m. – 8 p.m.
B **7.** Safe in room for valuables.
Y **8.** 11 p.m. curfew.
Y **9.** 10% discount for members.
H **10.** Call 0 for room service.

2 Conversation

A

[CD 1, Track 17]

Answers
An important rule at the hostel is "You can't make noise after midnight."
Guests can use the kitchen any time, and they can drink coffee and tea in the lobby all day.

B

Answers
Jun: Oh, sure. 1
Manager: You can't make noise after midnight. 4
Manager: Yes….You're allowed to use the kitchen any time. 3
Manager: Yes…Here is your key. 2

Page 15

3 Language Booster

A

Have students use *not OK* to talk about something that is not allowed and use *permitted* to talk about something allowed. (For example, It's not OK to play music loudly. You are permitted to play music, but only quietly.)

4 Listening

A

[CD 1, Track 18]

Answers	
1. b	**3.** c
2. e	**4.** d

B

[CD 1, Track 18]

Answers
Answers will vary.
1. You can park anywhere. / You can't park in front of the building.
2. You aren't allowed to have parties on weekdays. / It's OK to have parties on the weekend, but you must finish by midnight.
3. You are permitted to have guests, but they can't get a key.
4. It's OK to have pets, but not dogs.

C

Example conversation

A: In my neighborhood, we can't park our bikes on the sidewalk.

B: In my neighborhood, we aren't allowed to park our cars unless we have a special sticker. It shows we've gotten permission to park in a certain place.

5 Speak with Confidence

B

Example conversation

A: We think it's good to have a rule that we can only speak English.

B: We agree, but we don't think there should be a fine.

Lesson 7 There are some problems.

Page 16
1 Vocabulary

A

Answers	
1. d	**5.** b
2. e	**6.** h
3. g	**7.** f
4. c	**8.** a

Optional Activity

Have students get into pairs and rank the complaints from most important to fix to least important to fix right away.

Example conversation

A: I think the toilet not flushing is the most important problem to fix right away.

B: I agree. Without a toilet, you can't stay in the room.

A: No hot water is the second most important problem. Sometimes it takes time to fix that kind of problem.

2 Conversation

A

[CD 1, Track 19]

Answers
The lamp by the bed isn't working. The faucet is leaking. There aren't any towels. The hotel clerk says he will have housekeeping bring some towels right away.

Optional Question

What does *send* in *I'll ask housekeeping to send you some now* mean? (It means *bring*.)

C

[CD 1, Track 20]

Answers
Additional sentences underlined. Guest: Hi…There are some problems with my room. <u>I'm in room 429.</u> Guest: That's what I thought. And the faucet in the bathroom is leaking. <u>I can't turn it off.</u> Guest: Great. I really appreciate it. <u>Thanks very much.</u>

Optional Activity

Have students talk about how they would feel if they had just checked into a room with all of these problems.

Page 17
4 Pronunciation

A

[CD 1, Track 21]

Point out that the /d/ in *and* becomes silent.

B

Answers
Answers will vary. Sample answer. 1. toilet 2. lamp 3. soup

5 Speak with Confidence

A

Answers
Answers will vary. Sample answer. 1. There's no remote control. 2. There aren't any sheets on the bed. 3. There is no lightbulb in the lamp. 4. There is trash in the room. 5. There is a mouse on the floor!

B

Example conversation

A: Hello. This is Adam Smith in room 13. The room has not been cleaned.

B: Let me get someone to come and clean it.

A: Actually, I'd prefer to change rooms. The toilet is also leaking.

B: I'm sorry. There are no other rooms available. I'll get someone to come and look at the toilet, too.

A: The sheets are missing too, and there's no remote control.

B: I'll get someone to bring a remote control and new sheets. So, are you happy with these solutions?

A: No, I'm not!

Lesson 8 That would be great.

Page 18
1 Vocabulary

A

Answers			
1. b		**5.** g	
2. f		**6.** d	
3. e		**7.** a	
4. h		**8.** c	

B

Example conversation

A: A restaurant server might tell us the daily specials, like the food the chef recommends that day or the food they only have that day.

B: And a server would probably refill our water glasses.

2 Conversation

A
[CD 1, Track 22]

Answers
Laura wants to go to the museum and the mountains. The tourist information agent is going to mail the postcards for Laura.

B

Answers
Laura: Hi. Do you have a city map? 4
Agent: Yes. A tour bus company does that. 1
Laura: That sounds great. 3
Laura: Sure. I'd appreciate that. 2

Optional Activity

Have students think of other sentences to substitute for numbers 1-4 and then practice again. For example:

1. The tour starts at 9:30 every morning.

2. Have a great day!

3. Could you make a reservation for me?

4. I've never been here before.

Page 19
3 Language Booster

B

Example conversation

A: Would you like me to get your car?

B: That would be great.

4 Listening

A
[CD 1, Track 23]

Answers			
4. a		**3.** d	
_ b		**1.** e	
2. c		**5.** f	

B
[CD 1, Track 23]

Answers
1. check on the passenger's connecting (next) flight
2. get his car
3. wrap the gift
4. bring a dessert menu
5. change the guest's (hotel) room

Optional Activity

Have students get into pairs and practice the conversations by using the audio scripts at the back of their books (page 101).

5 Speak with Confidence

Answers
Answers will vary. Sample answers.
Movie time: Would you like me to look it up on the Internet?
I can call and find out if you'd like.
Directions to the party: I can draw you a map.
I'd be happy to show you.
Didn't do homework: I can let you turn it in late.
Would you like me to help you do it quickly?
Dead cell phone battery: Would you like to use my phone?
Do you want me to charge it for you?
Really hungry: I'd be happy to go get you something to eat.
I can get you a snack if you like.

Lessons 5 to 8 Review

English in Action

Page 20

1 Preview

A

> **Answers**
>
> **Answers will vary.** Sample answer.
> Maria and Jill are at their hotel.
> They are checking into the hotel. They might be
> complaining about a problem.

2 Practice

A

> **Answers**
>
> 1. Jill's last name is spelled Willcox.
> 2. Jill hands the clerk her driver's license and her credit card.
> 3. Tea and coffee are in the room.
> 4. They can't make noise after midnight, and parties are not allowed.

B

> **Answers**
>
> 1. The light in their room isn't working, so they can't see anything.

3   Discuss

Example conversation

A: Do people ever have problems spelling or saying your name?

B: Yes, all the time.

C: Do you usually correct them?

B: The first time or two, but after that, I just give up.

A: Do you think it is OK for a hotel to ask that there be no parties?

D: Yes, because parties can get really loud and bother other people.

A: I agree. Does anyone disagree?

B: No. So, have you ever lost power?

C: Yes. We went to my friend's house for three days until the power was back on.

Speak Now

Page 21

Provide an example of each conversation when necessary. If many students need more practice with a particular unit, you might want to review it in class.

5 *Example conversation*

A: Hello. I'd like to check in.

B: Do you have a reservation?

A: Yes. The name is Anderson.

B: Here it is. You're staying four nights in a double room. Is that correct?

A: Yes.

B: OK. Please fill out this form. And may I have your passport and credit card please?

6 *Example conversation*

A: Welcome to ALL GYM. Let me just mention some of the rules. First, you're not allowed to eat food in the gym. Please eat in the restaurant.

B: Where's the restaurant?

A: On the second floor. And no one is permitted to bring guests to the gym without a pass. If you have a guest, please bring them to the desk first.

7 *Example conversation*

A: Excuse me, my steak is cold.

B: I'm very sorry. I'll have a new one brought to you right away.

A: And there's no butter for the bread.

B: I'll have the server bring you some.

8 *Example conversation*

A: Do you want me to mail these letters?

B: That won't be necessary.

A: Would you like me to get you a newspaper?

B: Sure. I'd appreciate that.

A: I'd be happy to call a taxi for you.

B: That's OK. I can walk.

Lesson 9 Do you know…?

Page 22
1 Vocabulary

A

Answers			
1. g	**3.** h	**5.** a	**7.** d
2. f	**4.** b	**6.** c	**8.** e

Optional Activity

Have students get into pairs and practice the questions, making answers to go with them.

Answers
Answers will vary. Sample answer for optional activity.
1. Those TVs over there.   5. Yes, they are organic.
2. I'm sorry. That's the only color we have left.   6. About 45 minutes.
7. No, you don't.
3. What is it?   8. Yes, it does. Which drink would you like?
4. Over there, next to the ink.

B

Answers
Answers will vary. Sample answer
a. organic food   **f.** expensive, unique, or designer clothing
b. paper, ink, folders
c. haircuts   **g.** TVs, MP3 players, computers
d. airline tickets, tours
e. fast food   **h.** cleaning clothes, removing stains

2 Conversation

A
[CD 1, Track 24]

Answers
Anne doesn't like that there is a lot of construction in her town.
Mark needs to get a haircut this weekend.

C
[CD 1, Track 25]

Answers
Additional sentences underlined.
Anne: Oh, it is. …But I really like it, and everything I need is close by. And my neighbors are friendly.
Anne: I don't think so. A haircut is $20 or so. That's reasonable.
Anne: It's next to Super Foods. You can take a bus there. There's one every 20 minutes.

Page 23
3 Language Booster

A

Optional Activity

Have students make indirect questions for each of the examples.

How much is the bus?

What bus do I need?

Where can I get a haircut?

Is it expensive?

Do the buses run late?

Can I use a credit card?

Have students make rules for forming indirect questions. For example, move *can* to before the verb. *Be* verbs are at the end of indirect questions, unless the question has an *if* clause. With an *if* clause, the *be* verb is after the subject (for example, it's). The *do* is replaced by *if*.

4 Pronunciation

A
[CD 1, Track 26]

Emphasize to students that they should not use falling intonation with these questions. Explain that if they use falling intonation, the listener will think the speaker is demanding an answer rather than truly asking a question.

B

Example conversation

A: Do you know if it's expensive?

B: Sorry. I have no idea.

5 Speak with Confidence

A

Answers
Answers will vary. Sample answer.
1. where the nearest food court is
2. if there is a bus to the airport
3. the cheapest way to get to New York City
4. if I can buy DVDs at the electronics store

Lesson 10 Sorry. My mistake.

Page 24

1 Vocabulary

A

Answers	
1. receipt	4. overcharged
2. missing	5. misspelled
3. change	6. undercharged

B

Example conversation

A: I had to ask the bus driver for the correct change last week.

B: What happened?

A: He gave me a dollar back, but he owed me five.

2 Conversation

A

[CD 1, Track 27]

Answers
The customer gave the clerk $50.
The customer got back $10.

Optional Question

How much change should the customer have gotten? ($15)

B

Answers
Customer: Yes. 3
Clerk: Really? 1
Clerk: Right. 4
Clerk: Oh, I'm sorry…I thought there were three bills there. 2

Page 25

3 Language Booster

A

Point out that the mistake (i.e., the problem on the right side of the vertical line) can be stated without the phrase on the left. Tell students that adding the phrase on the left (for example, *I'm afraid*) makes the statement more polite.

4 Listening

A

[CD 1, Track 28]

Answers	
a. 2	c. 4
b. 3	d. 1

B

[CD 1, Track 28]

Answers
1. He promises to bring the correct bill and credit card.
2. He says he'll bring the correct order and give the man a free dessert.
3. He tells the customer to keep the extra ($1) change.
4. He says he'll bring a new bill that doesn't have the dessert charged twice.

Optional Activity

Have students listen again and write down how Frank apologized.

Answers
1. I'm so sorry.
2. My apologies.
3. Instead of directly apologizing, he says, "Please just keep it" about the extra change.
4. Please accept my apologies.

5 Speak with Confidence

Example conversation

A: Excuse me. The price on this item was $15, but you charged me $18.

B: Oh, I'm sorry. Let me give you the extra change.

Lesson 11 Can I please…?

Page 26

1 Vocabulary

A

Answers	
1. e	5. g
2. c	6. b
3. f	7. d
4. a	8. h

2 Conversation

A

[CD 1, Track 29]

Answers
Heather's appointment is on Friday the 20th at 3:30. She should arrive at 3:15.

C

[CD 1, Track 30]

Answers
Additional sentences underlined. Receptionist: Good morning. Dr. Kim's office. How can I help you? Heather: Um… I'd prefer something in the afternoon. I work in the morning. Receptionist: Would you be able to come in on Friday at 3:30? Are you free then?

Page 27

3 Language Booster

A

Tell students that they can replace *Can I* with *Could I* or *May I* to make more formal requests.

B

Example conversation

A: Can I make an appointment with a hairstylist to get my hair colored?

B: Certainly. What time are you free?

A: 1:00.

B: And your name?

A: Rachel Peppernut.

B: OK, Rachel, we'll see you at 1:00 this afternoon.

4 Pronunciation

A

[CD 1, Track 31]

- Tell students that the last sound in the first word is replaced with the first sound of the next word, so /m/ is repeated in *lemme* and *gimme*.

- Ask students to guess how they would reduce *want me*, providing the answer if necessary (*wamme*). Provide an example such as *Do you wamme to take a message?*

5 Speak with Confidence

A

Answers	
Answers will vary. Sample answer.	
a hairstylist	I need a haircut.
a dentist	My tooth hurts.
a doctor	I have a fever.
a career counselor	I don't like my job and want a new one.

B

Example conversation

A: I'd like to make an appointment. My hair is too long.

B: OK. Can you come in tomorrow at 2:00?

A: Certainly.

B: Great. To confirm, you are getting a haircut tomorrow at 2:00. [Student writes A's name, *hair too long*, and *2:00* in chart.]

C

Example conversation

A: I made appointment for today at 3:00, tomorrow at 2:00, and the day after tomorrow at 4:00. I'm going to get a haircut, see the dentist, and talk to a career counselor.

Lesson 12 I'm broke.

Page 28
1 Vocabulary

A

Answers	
1. d or f	**5.** g
2. a	**6.** h
3. b	**7.** d or f
4. c	**8.** e

2 Conversation

A

[CD 1, Track 32]

Answers
Calvin and Ben are going to save money by eating at home more often and going to fewer movies.

B

Answers
Calvin: We still need some more money for our trip to Italy. 2 Calvin: One thing we should do is to stop our gym memberships for a few months. 4 Ben: That's a good idea, but I go to the gym every day. We could eat at home instead of going out to eat so much. 3 Calvin: How about spending less on movies, too? 1

Remind students that eye contact is important in English-speaking countries and encourage students to use eye contact as they practice the conversation.

Page 29
3 Language Booster

B

Example conversation

A: I'm angry at my friend. What should I do?

B: One thing you could do is talk to her about why.

A: That's a good idea, but I'm not sure she will listen.

B: Well, something else you could do is send her an e-mail explaining the problem.

4 Listening

A

[CD 1, Track 33]

Answers			
_	1.	_	6.
✓	2.	✓	7.
_	3.	_	8.
✓	4.	✓	9.
✓	5.		

B

[CD 1, Track 33]

Answers
Students should underline the following suggestions: 2 5

C

Example conversation

A: What do you think of the recommendations in part A?

B: I think cancelling magazine subscriptions is a good idea, but I couldn't follow it. I love following the fashion news too much.

A: I think walking when possible is a good idea. I think I could do that.

5 Speak with Confidence

A

Example conversation

A: One thing we can do is watch movies on our computers instead of going to the movie theater. I think that's a good idea, but I want to go to a few movies in the theater.

B: I agree. It's a good idea, but for a special treat, it's nice to go to the theater.

B

Example conversation

A: Another thing we could do to save money on entertainment is to play games.

B: And we thought about trying to do more fun, free things outside.

C: I think that's the best idea.

Lessons 9 to 12 Review

English in Action

Page 30

1 Preview

A

Answers
Answers will vary. Sample answer. Students should check two of the places.

Optional Activity

Have students get into pairs and compare answers.

2 Practice

A

Answers
1. The hotel clerk says they should talk a walk in Central Park.
2. The hotel clerk says the prices in the East Village are cheaper than the rest of the city.
3. The hotel clerk suggests they go to Times Square at night.
4. The hotel clerk thinks it's fun to shop in Soho.

Optional Questions

Do Eric and Tom like Maria's new hair style? (No, they don't.)

Does Jill like Maria's new hair style? (Yes, she does.)

B

Example conversation

A: The hotel clerk tells Jill and Maria to take a walk in Central Park and to go to Times Square at night.

B: She also says that the prices in the East Village are cheap and to go to Soho for shopping.

3 Discuss

If some students are doing most of the talking, stop the discussion. Remind students that they can include everyone in the group by asking the quieter students their opinions (for example, by asking *How about you?*)

Speak Now

Page 31

Make sure students mark how well they can do each task. If many students need more practice with a particular unit, review it in class.

9 *Example conversation*

A: Tell me about your hometown. Do you know where I can buy some good gifts?

B: I'd go to the department store next to the train station.

10 *Example conversation*

A: Excuse me, but I think you gave me the wrong change. It was $14, and I gave you $20. But you only gave me $5.

B: Oh, I'm sorry. Here's the other dollar.

11 *Example conversation*

B: Photos Are Us. May I help you?

A: Yes. I'd like to make an appointment to have my photo taken.

B: Certainly. Would tomorrow at 3:00 work?

A: Yes.

B: Great. So your appointment will be with Kim tomorrow at 3:00. See you then.

12 *Example conversation*

A: I want to save money. What should I do?

B: You could stop your gym membership. You never go anyway.

A: That's a good idea.

B: Something else you could do is eat out a little less often. Cooking your own meals saves a lot of money.

A: I'm not so sure I like that idea.

Lesson 13 I used to play hopscotch.

Page 32

1 Vocabulary

A

Answers. Students' additional answers are in bold.
Places: playground, zoo, **skate park** People: bully, tomboy, **referee** Games: checkers, hopscotch, **tag**

Optional Activity

Have students brainstorm more places (for example, summer camp, swimming pool), people (for example, camp counselor, lifeguard, swimming instructor), and games (for example, hide-and-seek, board games, card games) from their childhood.

2 Conversation

A

[CD 1, Track 34]

Answers
Max and his friends sang karaoke and pretended they were on TV. Zoe was a tomboy. She played baseball.

C

[CD 1, Track 35]

Answers
Additional sentences underlined. Zoe: What kind of childhood did you have, Max? <u>Were you happy?</u> Max: Lots of things…My friends and I would pretend we were on TV. <u>I was always the star!</u> Zoe: Oh, I was a tomboy! I used to play baseball. <u>Sometimes, I miss it.</u>

Page 33

3 Language Booster

A

- Explain that *used to* is used in sentences talking about something that was true in the past. Tell students that the action is either finished or no longer true.

- Point out that because *did* is in the past tense, *use to* is used. (i.e., There are not two past tense forms—*did* and *used to*—in the same sentence.)

Optional Activity

Tell students that we can use *would* to talk about past habits. For example:

When I was young, I used to go bowling every Saturday. When I was young, I would go bowling every Saturday.

Have students practice again using *would*.

4 Pronunciation

A

[CD 1, Track 36]

- Emphasize that the pronunciation of *used to* and *use to* is exactly the same.

- Point out that both are formed with the present tense verb after *to*.

- To give students more practice, have them make multiple sentences, replacing hopscotch with other activities.

5 Speak with Confidence

A

Example conversation

A: Did you use to have an unusual nickname as a child?

B: Yes.

A: How did you get it?

B: My little brother couldn't say my name correctly, and after that, everyone started using that as my nickname.

[Student A writes B's name and *from little brother*]

B

Example conversation

A: I found out B's little brother couldn't say his name, and because of that, he got his nickname.

B: I found out D is good at math, but when she was little, she wasn't very good at it.

Lesson 14 She said she was sorry.

Page 34

1 Vocabulary

A

Answers	
1. d	**5.** f
2. a	**6.** g
3. e	**7.** c
4. b	

B

Example conversation

A: I wore two different color socks all day and didn't realize it.

B: How embarrassing! How did you finally realize it?

A: I bent down to tie my shoe and noticed it.

2 Conversation

A

[CD 1, Track 37]

Answers
Alex's friend wanted an autograph of Rihanna. Alex was embarrassed because the woman wasn't really Rihanna.

B

Answers
Alex: Something really embarrassing happened to me on Saturday. I was having dinner with a friend at Lulu's. 3
Alex: Yeah, they do. Anyway, I saw someone famous at the next table—Rihanna! 1
Carrie: No way!…She has a fantastic voice. 2
Carrie: How embarrassing! 4

Page 35

3 Language Booster

A

Have students make rules about how to report what someone said. For example:

- *I* becomes the person's name or he/she. For example, *I* becomes *she*.
- Present tense verbs become past tense verbs. For example, *they have* becomes *they had*.
- Past actions that are finished use the past perfect tense. For example, *arrived* becomes *had arrived*.
- The future tense *will* becomes *would*.

B

Example conversation

A: My mother told me that she was planning to go to Paris to learn to speak French.

B: How romantic!

4 Listening

A

[CD 1, Track 38]

Answers	
1. F	**4.** F
2. F	**5.** T
3. F	

B

[CD 1, Track 38]

Answers
Answers will vary. Sample answer.
1. Inez told Chelsea she had won an online contest.
2. Inez said the prize was a trip to Paris.
3. Inez said she doesn't remember entering the contest.
4. She said the trip would be for one week.

C

Example conversation

A: Have you ever had something lucky happen to you?

B: Yes. Once I lost my cell phone in the woods, but I went back later and found it!

5 Speak with Confidence

B

Example conversation

A: I am very good at baseball.

B: He said he is very good at baseball.

C: He said he is a very good ball.

A: My sentence was a little different!

Lesson 15 I read an unusual story.

Page 36

1 Vocabulary

A

Answers	
1. denies	6. saves
2. breaks	7. cancels
3. causes	8. closes
4. crashes	9. catches
5. donates	10. scores

B

Example conversation

A: The story about the fan catching a baseball interests me. And I'm interested in the network cancelling all the reality shows. I'm not interested in any of the other stories.

2 Conversation

A

[CD 1, Track 39]

Answers
Cameron Titus is a 10-year-old boy who wrote a children's book. He has donated money to the charity, Habitat for Humanity.

Optional Activity

Tell students this is a true story. Have them talk about what they think *Cameron's A-Z* is about, and then tell them the book has a tongue twister for each letter of the alphabet.

C

[CD 1, Track 40]

Answers
Additional sentences underlined. Molly: Really? That's fantastic. Aaron: The towns near him had some bad storms. He wanted to help, so he donated all the money he made to the charity, Habitat for Humanity. They build homes. Molly: What a great kid. And generous, too!

Page 37

3 Language Booster

A

Point out that when talking about news, we often ask someone if they have read the same story (for example, Did you see the story about…?)

4 Pronunciation

A

[CD 1, Track 41]

- Tell students that the symbol /ə/ is pronounced schwa.
- Tell students that that the schwa sound can be spelled with any vowel letter or letters. (i.e., The schwa is not associated with a specific vowel.)
- Remind students that they are practicing examples of the schwa being reduced in unstressed syllables.

B

[CD 1, Track 42]

Answers			
1. children	2. local	3. second	4. cancel

5 Speak with Confidence

A

Example conversation

A: Let's do the singer story. The popular pop star said she is getting married next week.

B: And she plans to start a family.

A: She said she may start singing again in five or ten years, but for now, she's done singing.

B

Example conversation

A: We chose the singer story.

B: The popular pop star said she is getting married next week. And she plans to start a family. She said she may start singing again in five or ten years, but for now, she's done singing.

C: We chose the actor story.

D: Tony Lee said he didn't do anything special, but the parents certainly disagree.

B: How did he save the child?

Lesson 16 When did they release it?

Page 38

Optional Activity

Before students open their books, ask them to talk about how often they listen to or read the news (for example, every day), and what kinds of stories they pay attention to (for example, sports news).

Page 38

1 Vocabulary

A

Answers	
1. b	**5.** f
2. a	**6.** d
3. c	**7.** g
4. e	

B

Example conversation

A: What do you think the top news story was last year?

B: I think it was the royal wedding.

2 Conversation

A
[CD 1, Track 43]

Answers
The first Harry Potter film was released in 2001. Glen didn't get any questions correct.

B

Answers
Glen: I'm ready for Friday's current events quiz. 3
Allie: So, let me quiz you. When did Spain beat the Netherlands at the World Cup finals? 1
Glen: That's easy. It was in 2012. Next question. 2
Glen: I think the first one was in 2008. 4

Page 39

3 Language Booster

A

- Remind students that we use *in* when the time period is not specific (i.e., *in month, in year*), but we use *on* when the date is specific (i.e., *on month day, year*).

- Point out that we don't use *happen* to ask about when things happened. Instead, we use specific verbs (for example, *host, release, get married*).

Optional Activity

- Have students get into small groups. Give each group one topic (for example, sports, technology, famous people). Have each group make five questions about that topic. The questions should be increasingly difficult, with students assigning 100, 200, 300, 400, and 500 points to the questions. You may want to have students make multiple choice answers.

- When students have finished making their questions, write the topics on the board, with 100-500 points under each.

- Have groups take turns selecting a topic and level of difficulty. The team that made the question asks, and if the other group answers correctly, that group gets the points. Play continues as time allows, or until all of the questions have been used.

- The winner is the team with the most points.

4 Listening

A

Answers	
Answers will vary. Sample answer.	
1. b	**3.** b
2. a	**4.** c

B
[CD 1, Track 44]

Answers
1. a   **2.** a   **3.** b   **4.** a
Answers to the final question will vary.
Yes, I did. / No, I didn't.

Optional Questions

How much money could Walter have won? ($1 million)

How much money did Walter win? ($0. / No money.)

Lessons 13 to 16 Review

English in Action

Page 40

1 Preview

A

Answers
Answers will vary for first question. Sample answer.

I think Tom and Eric's apartment is really messy and they can't find anything.

a. 3
b. 2
c. 1
d. 4

2 Practice

A

Answers
Answers will vary. Sample answer.
Yes, I did. / No, I didn't.

B

Answers
1. window
2. robbed
3. police
4. a teddy bear
5. the sofa

Optional Questions

What is Eric's teddy bear's name? (Brownie.)

Does Tom want to call the police? (No, probably because he's not certain they were robbed.)

Were they robbed? (No.)

3 Discuss

Example conversation

A: Do you still have anything special from your childhood?

B: I have some toys from Germany and Egypt. My grandparents gave them to me when they went there.

C: Cool! What's the most valuable thing you own?

D: My computer. I couldn't live without it. How about you? Do you still have anything special from your childhood?

Speak Now

Page 41

In a mixed-ability class, have lower-level students make the required conversations but encourage higher level students to provide reasons for their answers and expand the conversation (i.e., don't just follow a Question-Answer, Question-Answer, trade partners, Question-Answer, Question-Answer pattern).

13 *Example conversation*

A: What games did you use to play as a kid?

B: I used to play tag and hide-and-seek.

14 *Example conversation*

A: My mother told me not to be late for dinner because she was making pizza, and my father said he would be late, so we should start without him. My mother also said that I should bring a friend home for dinner.

B: Is your mother's pizza good?

A: It's the best! Do you want to join us?

15 *Example conversation*

A: I saw a story about a woman who won the lottery. So many people asked her for money that she had to move.

B: Really?

A: Yeah. But then later she lost all of the money in the stock market.

B: That's interesting.

16 *Example conversation*

A: How old were you when you got your first cell phone?

B: Ten.

A: When did you move to our city?

B: I moved here in 2011.

A: That's right. I remember now. And when did you win your first English speech contest?

B: In 2012.

Lesson 17 You didn't know?

Page 42
1 Vocabulary

A

Answers	
1. d	**5.** f
2. b	**6.** c
3. a	**7.** g
4. e	

B

Example conversation

A: I think the best type of friend is a lifelong friend.

B: I think a best friend is the best kind of friend, because you can tell him anything.

A: The worst type of friend is a fair-weather friend.

B: I totally agree.

2 Conversation

A
[CD 2, Track 2]

Answers
Kal calls Winnie to ask her advice about his relationship with his best friend, Brad. Winnie saw Brad working at a coffee shop.

Point out the question *Do you have a minute?* Tell students this is a polite way to start a phone conversation. It tells the other person that if the speaker called at a bad time, he/she will call later.

C
[CD 2, Track 3]

Answers
Additional sentences underlined. Kal: Hi, it's Kal…It's about my best friend Brad. You know him, right? Kal: Of course. Go ahead. Kal: He did? I had no idea.

Page 43
3 Language Booster

B

Example conversation

A: My close friends and I like to play soccer on the weekends.

B: You do? I thought you worked on Saturdays and Sundays.

4 Pronunciation

A
[CD 2, Track 4]

- Tell students that this intonation is very important. Explain that if they use falling intonation, the listener may think the speaker is agreeing rather than showing surprise or interest.

- Tell students that generally when showing surprise, the rising intonation goes higher than when showing interest.

- Explain that when showing surprise, the speed of the last word is often slowed down (for example, You a-r-e?).

B

Answers
Answers will vary. Sample answer.   **1.** ignore the call   **2.** fine   **3.** lots of friends

C

Example conversation

A: I would answer the phone if a friend called me at 3 a.m.

B: You would?

5 Speak with Confidence

B

Example conversation

A: I've known my three closest friends since I started elementary school

B: You have?

C: Did you go to high school together, too?

Lesson 18 A good friend is loyal.

Page 44

1 Vocabulary

A

Answers	
1. supportive	5. forgiving
2. loyal	6. caring
3. truthful	7. reliable
4. accepting	

B

Example conversation

A: I think I'm loyal and supportive.

B: And I think you're accepting, too.

2 Conversation

A

[CD 2, Track 5]

Answers
Hugh likes friends who are truthful and don't say things behind your back. For Jo, it's important to be reliable.

B

Answers
Jo: Have you made many friends since you moved here, Hugh? 3 Hugh: I've actually made quite a few friends. 2 Jo: What sort of people do you like to be friends with? 4 Hugh: To me, it's important for a friend to be truthful. You know—they don't say things behind your back and stuff. 1

Page 45

3 Language Booster

B

Example conversation

A: What's important to you in a friend?

B: It's important for a friend to be forgiving. How about you?

A: The most important thing is how reliable someone is.

4 Listening

A

[CD 2, Track 6]

Answers
1. T
2. F (The man's friend Casey didn't agree that his sister was acting silly. / The man's friend Casey helped him realize he was being insensitive.)
3. F (The woman was upset because her friends didn't call, send cards, or come see her when she was in the hospital.)
4. F (The man and Patrick grew apart, and this made the man sad.)

Optional Activity

Have students correct the false statements. (Answers above.)

Optional Questions

Was the first woman surprised Jonathan got upset? (Yes. She thought he wouldn't mind if she paid the money back a week later.)

Does the third woman think it's more important to have many friends or real friends? (She thinks it's more important to have real friends.)

B

[CD 2, Track 6]

Answers	
1. b	3. d
2. a	4. c

Optional Activity

Have students talk about other proverbs about friends. (For example, a German proverb says, "The death of a friend is equivalent (equal) to the loss of a limb."

5 Speak with Confidence

B

Example conversation

A: I think a parent should be forgiving, reliable, and supportive.

B: But a parent needs to be caring and accepting, too.

C: And a parent must be loving. It's hard to choose only three important qualities.

Lesson 19 I could do that.

Page 46
1 Vocabulary

A

Answers
Answers will vary. Sample answer. G take a class G make friends through friends G play sports B introduce yourself to people G do volunteer work B join an online group G join a student club G go to social events G use social networks

2 Conversation

A

[CD 2, Track 7]

Answers
Rod doesn't like Carrie's first suggestion because he likes to meet people face to face (in person). He doesn't like her second suggestion because he would feel strange introducing himself to others.

B

Answers
Carrie: You should join an online group. 3 Rod: That doesn't appeal to me. I prefer to meet people face to face. 4 Rod: I'd feel strange doing that. 2 Carrie: I know! Why not join my dance class? 1

Page 47
4 Listening

A

[CD 2, Track 8]

Answers
1. (I think you should) join a class. 2. (You should just) introduce yourself to people at parties, in the cafeteria, and places like that. 3. (Have you thought about) doing volunteer work? 4. (If you want to make friends, you should) play sports. 5. (I'd) join a student club.

Optional Activity

Have students get into pairs and talk about which suggestions they agree and disagree with, giving reasons for their answers.

Example conversation

A: I don't agree with joining a student club because you'll only meet other students. Doing volunteer work lets you meet all kinds of people.

B: That's true, but you can't hang out with someone who is much older than you. Meeting other students is a good idea.

B

[CD 2, Track 8]

Answers	Positively	Negatively
1.	✓	
2.		✓
3.	✓	
4.		✓
5.	✓	

Optional Activity

Have students listen to the first two conversations again. Who is Abigail talking with? How do you know?

Answers
1. a friend, because he laughs when she says she still likes her current friends (which would include him) 2. a friend who is also friends with John

5 Speak with Confidence

B

Example conversation

A: I spend time with my friends. You can't maintain a friendship if you don't spend time together.

B: I agree. Keeping in touch regularly is important. But if you want to keep a friendship, you shouldn't talk behind your friend's back.

C: I agree with both of you. If you want to be friends, you have to trust each other.

Lesson 20 I wish I'd remembered.

Page 48
1 Vocabulary

A

Answers	
1. Apologize	4. feelings
2. involved	5. problem
3. Ignore	6. joke

2 Conversation

A
[CD 2, Track 9]

Answers
Brett forgot the party because he was busy all week. Dana suggests Brett call John and apologize. She also suggests Brett be honest about what happened.

C
[CD 2, Track 10]

Answers
Additional sentences underlined. Brett: You'll never guess what happened. My friend John invited me to a party at his house last night, and I totally forgot about it. I feel awful. Dana: Have you talked to him? Was he upset? Brett: Not yet. I don't know what to do. What do you think?

Optional Activity

Have students get into pairs and discuss a time they forgot someone's birthday or another special event, or when someone forgot their birthday.

Example conversation

A: Once, I went home from college for the weekend, and it was my birthday. My dad spent the whole morning as if it wasn't my birthday.

B: How awful. What did you do?

A: I didn't do anything. Later, he was on the phone and said, "Today? Oh!" He looked over at me. When he got off the phone, he apologized.

B: I guess parents are human, too.

A: Yeah. How about you? Has anyone every forgotten your birthday?

Page 49
3 Language Booster

B

Example conversation

A: The other day my friend was 30 minutes late. We were supposed to go to a movie, but we missed it because she was late. I told her how angry I was, and now, we aren't talking. I wish I hadn't gotten so upset.

B: One thing you can do is call her and apologize.

4 Pronunciation

A
[CD 2, Track 11]

Tell students that to link two /n/, /s/, /l/, or /m/ sounds they should speak smoothly (i.e., with an unbroken stream of air coming from their mouths).

5 Speak with Confidence

Example conversation

A: I think Bob may have done the right thing, because he didn't know the truth. But once he found out the truth, he should have apologized to Julia.

B: But he could have talked with Julia first, and asked her about it before he said she should pay for the damage.

C: I think Tim did the right thing. If he hadn't talked to Matt, he would have felt bad.

D: Yeah. It would have hurt their relationship, because Matt didn't really say anything bad.

Lessons 17 to 20 Review

English in Action

Page 50

1 Preview

Answers
Answers will vary. Sample answer. They should apologize, get a birthday cake, and sing *Happy Birthday* to Tom.

2 Practice

A

Answers
1. T
2. F   Yesterday was Tom's birthday.
3. T
4. F   Jill suggests they apologize, and Eric agrees.
5. F   They buy Tom pasta for his birthday.

B

Have students rewrite the false answers to make them true. Answers above.

Optional Questions

Does Jill think Tom is an acquaintance? (No. She said he's not just an acquaintance, meaning he is a friend.)

Who suggests they lie to Tom? (Maria does.)

What is Tom's second favorite thing? (Surprises.)

3 Discuss

Example conversation

A: Have you ever forgotten someone's special day?

B: Yeah. One time I forgot my sister's birthday. Luckily my mom called to remind me that night. I called my sister and she never found out.

C: That was pretty lucky. Have you ever been to a surprise party?

D: Yeah. My friend Curtis had a surprise birthday party for our friend Darrin. It was really fun. How about you, Jan? Have you ever forgotten someone's special day?

E: I forget my parents' anniversary all the time.

Speak Now

Page 51

Provide an example of each conversation when necessary.

17 *Example conversation*

A: I first met my friend Becky in Thailand.

B: You did? Why were you both in Thailand?

A: We were doing volunteer work. That was about five years ago.

B: It was?

A: Yeah, and we still like to do volunteer work together.

B: You do? What have you done recently?

18 *Example conversation*

A: What's important to be a good friend?

B: It's important to respect your friend.

A: Is that the most important quality?

B: The most important thing is probably compassion.

19 *Example conversation*

A: If you want to have less stress, you should exercise every day.

B: That sounds like a good idea, but I don't have much time.

A: You could also do something fun to relax—like play active video games.

B: I can see myself doing that.

20 *Example conversation*

A: I wish I hadn't told my friend she is always late. Now she won't talk to me.

B: One thing you can do is call her and apologize.

A: She won't answer the phone.

B: Something you might try is sending a card to tell her how sorry you are.

Lesson 21 I'd rather not say.

Page 52

1 Vocabulary

A

> **Answers**
>
> **Answers will vary.** Sample answer.
> **VI** leadership   **SI** overseas experience
> **VI** communication skills
> **VI** computer skills   **SI** good school grades
> **SI** knowledge of current affairs
> **VI** work experience   **SI** a graduate degree
> **VI** fluency in English

Optional Activity

Have students get into pairs and discuss their answers, giving reasons for their ideas.

Example conversation

A: I think leadership is very important. Companies need employees who set good examples.

B: And I think computer skills are also very important. Everything is on a computer these days.

2 Conversation

A

[CD 2, Track 13]

> **Answers**
>
> Emily thinks she is suitable for the job because she took courses at college and has work experience. She doesn't want to answer the question about why she worked at Mesa Design for only three months.

B

> **Answers**
>
> Emily: Well, I took two courses in marketing at college and really enjoyed them. 2
> Interviewer: I see that here. Why only three months? 1
> Emily: Um, I'd rather not say. I'll just say it wasn't the right company for me. 3
> Emily: Excellent. I can use all the main programs and I taught myself web design. 4

Optional Activity

Have students get into pairs and discuss whether they think Emily will get the job, giving reasons for their answers.

Example conversation

A: I think Emily will get the position, because even though she only stayed with Mesa Design for three months, she got a good reference.

B: That's true, but the interviewer may wonder if Emily will leave his firm after a short time, too.

Page 53

3 Language Booster

B

Example conversation

A: My communication skills are excellent.

B: I'm good at computers, and I also know how to explain problems so people who don't understand computers can follow what I am saying.

4 Listening

A

[CD 2, Track 14]

> **Answers**
>
> 5 **a.**   2 **d**
> 4 **b.**   3 **e.**
> 6 **c.**   1 **f.**

B

[CD 2, Track 14]

> **Answers**
>
> **Students' answers can be in note form.**
> **a.** People say that I have a lot of confidence. And that I'm very organized.
> **b.** X
> **c.** I think I work too hard and don't take enough time for myself.
> **d.** Actually, no. I have class in the morning, so I can only work in the afternoon.
> **e.** I'm good with computers and languages. I speak Spanish and a little Japanese.
> **f.** I'm a people person.

5 Speak with Confidence

B

If students are having problems imagining the Interviewer's role, have them refer to the Listening audio script on pages 110–111.

Lesson 22 It could be an ad for…

Page 54

1 Vocabulary

A

Answers	
1. f	**5.** c
2. e	**6.** a
3. d	**7.** b
4. g	

B

Example conversation

A: A long time ago I heard there was a slogan, "Where's the beef?"

B: "Reach out and touch someone" was a slogan for a phone company.

2 Conversation

A

[CD 2, Track 15]

Answers
John thinks the ad is for hair coloring.
Amanda says an effective ad should be simple and direct. She doesn't think an ad needs to say much.

Optional Activity

Have students talk about the slogans in Vocabulary and decide what makes each of them effective, giving reasons for their answers.

Example conversation

A: Everyone likes the idea that they can eat their food just like they like it—like they aren't just one person in a million.

B: That's true. And people like to think they have value, so "Because you're worth it" would appeal to many people.

C

[CD 2, Track 16]

Answers
Additional sentences underlined.
Amanda: I'm not sure. It looks like it could be for shampoo. Doesn't it?
John: Shampoo? Maybe. I think it's probably for hair coloring. I'm not sure.
Amanda: That's possible. Or I wonder if it's advertising cosmetics. It's hard to tell.

Page 55

3 Language Booster

A

- Tell students that the sentences describing probability and possibility are in order from most confidence in the statement to least confidence.

- Explain that *must* suggests the speaker is almost 100% certain.

- Tell students that *could* is used to discuss one of several possibilities, although often the other possibilities are unnamed. For example, it could be an ad for shampoo (but it could be an ad for hair coloring or cosmetics).

- Tell students we can also use *may* and *might* to show possibility. Because the speaker who uses *could* implies there are many possibilities, *could* statements are not as strong as those with *might* or *may*.

4 Pronunciation

A

[CD 2, Track 17]

- Tell students that /p/, /t/, and /k/ make a sudden pause, but /b/, /d/, and /g/ are less sudden, with a slightly shorter pause.

- Have students try holding sounds or slightly holding their breath to help them not pronounce the sounds as fully as they otherwise would.

B

Remind students that they should blend *what do you* so it sounds like *waddaya*.

5 Speak with Confidence

C

Example conversation

A: I think *Start your day the natural way* is the best slogan.

B: So do I. Everyone who agrees, please raise your hands. One, two, three. OK. Ten people agree.

C: And *Your way or no way* is awesome.

D: Does anyone else agree?

Lesson 23 The main reason is…

Optional Activity

Before students open their books, have them talk about their favorite shopping mall. Encourage them to talk about what makes it a good place to shop.

Page 56

1 Vocabulary

A

Answers
Some answers may vary. Sample answer.
1. b   4. d
2. c   5. f
3. a   6. e

B

Example conversation

A: Shopping malls could have fashion shows. They could also have live music.

B: Those are both good ideas. They could also have a babysitter so mothers can shop without worrying about their kids.

Optional Activity

Have students think about other kinds of businesses, for example, restaurants, and what those places could do to attract more customers. For example, a restaurant could have a special food menu that changes every day.

2 Conversation

A
[CD 2, Track 18]

Answers
Fewer people are buying books at Phil's bookstore because it's so easy to shop online.
He's brought in authors for book signings, and he's opened a coffee shop.

C
[CD 2, Track 19]

Answers
Additional sentences underlined.
Jan: How's the store doing, Phil? <u>It looks different.</u>
Jan: But why is that? <u>Are people reading less?</u>
Phil: Yes. And we've just opened this coffee shop. <u>Let's get a cup!</u>

Page 57

3 Language Booster

Point out that trends are often described by using comparative language such as *-er* and *as…as*.

4 Pronunciation

A
[CD 2, Track 20]

Point to the third example and remind students that spelling and pronunciation are often not related. Also point out that vowels can have the /w/ and /y/ sounds.

B
[CD 2, Track 21]

Answers
/w/	/y/	/w/	/y/

5 Speak with Confidence

B

Example conversation

A: Matthew and I think more and more college graduates are waiting before they get a job. Some of them are continuing their education, getting a Master's degree.

B: But I'm not sure that's by choice. It's hard to get a job these days. So maybe we don't agree on all the reasons for the trends.

C: Can we all agree that online shopping is becoming more and more popular?

D: I think it's due to the fact that it's so easy to compare many stores at once.

Lesson 24 It needs a good location.

Page 58

1 Vocabulary

A

Answers
location   service   prices   logo   marketing   idea

Optional Activity

Say the following adjectives and have students decide which noun(s) in Vocabulary they can describe. (Answers in parentheses.)

An original (idea, logo)

A prime (location)

Competitive (prices)

B

Example conversation

A: Zippidy Doo is really successful. I always have to wait in line.

B: I know! Yesterday I waited 25 minutes just to order my coffee—for take-out! I think another successful business is Home-and-Away. I heard they are booked up a year ahead. I think they're successful because they offer so many different places. You can compare them quickly and easily.

2 Conversation

A
[CD 2, Track 22]

Answers
Carmen thinks location, affordable prices, free wireless Internet, and quality coffee are important for starting a café.
She doesn't think an original idea is necessary.

B

Answers
Carmen: I really want to open my own café. 3
Carmen: It needs a good location, like near a school, so I can get business from students. 1
Carmen: Definitely. The prices have to be affordable. It must have free wireless Internet, too. 4
Carmen: Name? I haven't thought of one. 2

Optional Activity

Have students get into pairs and talk about what Carmen should name her café.

Example conversation

A: She could name it Carmen's.

B: But there might be a catchier name.

Page 59

3 Language Booster

B

Example conversation

A: What do you need to run a successful hair salon?

B: The prices have to be affordable, and it can't be too far out of the way.

4 Listening

A
[CD 2, Track 23]

Answers
1. T
2. F (Even the best location can't help a poorly run business.)
3. T
4. T

Optional Activity

Have students correct the false statement. (See answer above.)

B
[CD 2, Track 24]

Answers	
1. up-sell (sell things other than your main product)	**2.** keep costs down
3. pay your employees well

5 Speak with Confidence

B

Example conversation

A: We think a flower shop needs friendly service.

D: So do we. We also think the prices must be affordable.

Lessons 21 to 24 Review

English in Action

Page 60

1 Preview

Answers

Answers will vary. Sample answer.
1. Tom is wearing a suit and tie.
2. I think Tom is at a business office.
3. I think he's applying for a job.

2 Practice

A

Answers

Answers to first question will vary.
Yes, I did. / No, I didn't.
Students should write any three of the following:
1. confident
2. a hard worker
3. reliable
4. trustworthy
5. too focused

B

Answers

1. What makes you different?
2. How are you reliable and trustworthy?
3. What is your greatest weakness?
4. What is the reason?

Optional Activity

Ask students how they think Tom did. Would they have done anything differently?

3 Discuss

Example conversation

A: Have you ever had an interview?

B: Yes, I've had interviews for every job I've had.

C: How would you describe yourself?

D: I'm reliable, confident, and creative. So how about you? What can you say about your past experiences?

A: I think my past experiences have taught me how to be a better friend and person.

Speak Now

Page 61

21 *Example conversation*

A: So what do you think your strengths are?

B: I can speak five languages and learn new things quickly.

A: And what are your weaknesses?

B: I'd rather not say.

A: Do you have any experience?

B: Yes, I've worked in advertising for six years.

22 *Example conversation*

B: What do you think *the ultimate driving machine* is a slogan for?

A: It must be a slogan for a car. What do you think the next one is probably for?

B: *The best part of wakin' up?* It sounds like it could be a slogan for coffee or breakfast food.

23 *Example conversation*

A: In my hometown, bigger shopping malls are opening up, and small stores are closing.

B: Why?

A: The main reason is that it's so easy to go to many stores, all at once, when you go to a shopping mall. The small stores are spread across the city, so it takes time to go to several.

B: And malls sometimes have cheaper prices. What's another trend?

A: People are spending more time in libraries because books and magazines are so expensive. They can save a lot of money if they don't buy them.

24 *Example conversation*

A: What's necessary to run a clothing store?

B: It must have the latest fashions, but the prices have to be affordable.

A: What do you need to run a successful bakery?

B: A bakery needs a good location and delicious food.

Lesson 25 You're expected to…

Page 62

1 Vocabulary

A

Answers	
1. acknowledge	4. decline, Accept
2. pour	5. expected
3. bow, shake	

Optional Activity

Have students talk about how these customs are similar to and different than those in their countries.

B

Example conversation

A: In my country, at a formal dinner the most important person sits in front of the flower arrangement.

B: Really? In my country, you give other people your business card with both hands. Only using one hand is rude.

2 Conversation

A

[CD 2, Track 25]

Answers
Sarah told Dan to take off his shoes before going into homes, take a small gift when visiting homes, and do not open a gift right away.

C

[CD 2, Track 26]

Answers
Additional sentences underlined. Sarah: That's right. And when you visit someone's home, it's the custom to bring a small gift. Just don't give a clock. Dan: OK. That's good to know. Sarah: But in China, if someone gives you a gift, you're not supposed to open it right away. That would be very impolite.

Page 63

3 Language Booster

A

- Point out that each sentence has *to*, followed by a present tense verb.
- Tell students that the expectations are in order of force, with *expected to* showing more necessity than *polite to*.

4 Pronunciation

A

[CD 2, Track 27]

- Although it is important to divide sentences into thought groups, emphasize that students should not pause as if each group is an independent sentence. Doing so can be confusing and tiring for the listener.
- Tell students that we still emphasize the most important words in each thought group. Point out that this is often the last word in the thought group.

B

[CD 2, Track 28]

Answers			
Note the following words and syllables are stressed in the thought groups.			
expected	greet	oldest	first
custom	gift	visit	home

5 Speak with Confidence

A

Example conversation

A: In South Korea, everyone turns one year older on January 1st.

B: In Denmark, the country's flag is flown outside a window to show someone in that house is celebrating a birthday.

C: In Japan, boys who turn five go to a shrine in November of that year.

D: I heard that in Egypt, a birthday party is given for one-week-old babies. Do you think that's true?

Lesson 26 What does it mean?

Page 64
1 Vocabulary

A

Answers			
1. d	**2.** b	**3.** a	**4.** c
5. g	**6.** e	**7.** f	

B

Example conversation

A: Ignorance is bliss means what you don't know can't or won't hurt you.

B: Variety is the spice of life means lots of different things is more interesting than the same thing all the time.

2 Conversation

A

[CD 2, Track 29]

Answers
Emma really likes the proverb *Laughter is the best medicine.* It means finding something to laugh about even when things are hard.

B

Answers
Emma: I really like "*Laughter is the best medicine.*" 3 Emma: It reminds me to find humor during difficult times. 4 Emma: I think it means that the most important thing is to care for your own family. 1 Tomas: I'm trying to learn lots of proverbs, but it's taking me a long time. 2

Page 65
3 Language Booster

B

Example conversation

A: Love is blind. What does it mean to you?

B: I think it means that when people fall in love they only see the other person's good qualities.

4 Listening

A

Answers
Answers will vary. Sample answer. **a.** Think before you act. **b.** Something that is easy to get can also be easily lost. **c.** Don't judge people by how they look. **d.** People see what you do, so if your words and actions aren't the same, people will pay attention to your actions more than what you say. **e.** Two people had the same idea around the same time. **f.** It's in the past, so forget about it.

B

[CD 2, Track 30]

Answers			
3	**a.**	2	**d.**
5	**b.**	_	**e.**
1	**c.**	4	**f.**

Optional Activity

Have students look back at their guesses in Part A and revise the meanings of the proverbs, if necessary.

5 Speak with Confidence

A

Answers
Answers will vary. Sample answer. **1.** The nail that sticks up gets hammered down. **2.** If a job's worth doing, it's worth doing well. **3.** Have skin in the game.

B

Example conversation

A: There's a proverb, *The nail that sticks up gets hammered down.*

C: I think that means you shouldn't be different than other people.

B: That's right. What's one of your proverbs?

Lesson 27 What will happen if…?

Page 66

1 Vocabulary

A

Answers	
1. ladder	4. crack
2. coin	5. calendar
3. mirror	6. umbrella

B

Example conversation

A: It's good luck to find a penny.

B: Really? If you throw the penny into a fountain and make a wish, it will come true.

2 Conversation

A

[CD 2, Track 31]

Answers
The picture of the cat washing behind its ears is about the weather. The picture of the cat sneezing three times is about good luck.

B

Answers
Ann: If a cat washes behind its ears, it will rain soon. 4 Sam: I know another one about cats. What will happen if you see a white cat at night? 1 Ann: I wonder why. 3 Ann: Here's one. If a cat sneezes three times, you'll have good luck. 2

Page 67

3 Language Booster

A

- Point out that each question and consequence has *if*. If necessary, remind students that they use this grammar to talk about imaginary situations.

- Emphasize that they should use *will* with the result.

B

Example conversation

A: What will happen if you walk under a ladder?

B: You'll have bad luck.

4 Listening

A

[CD 2, Track 32]

Answers	
1. borrowed, blue	3. mirror, leaves
2. unlucky, dress	4. Friday, 13th

B

[CD 2, Track 32]

Answers	
Mark	**Lesley**
1. __	1. ✓
2. ✓	2. __
3. ✓	3. ✓
4. ✓	4. ✓

Optional Question

Which superstition had Lesley never heard of? (It's bad luck to look in a mirror *after* the bride leaves for the wedding ceremony.)

5 Speak with Confidence

A

Answers
Answers will vary. Sample answer. 1. A rabbit's foot will bring good luck. 2. If you find a four-leaf clover, you'll have good luck. 3. There is a pot of gold at the end of a rainbow.

B

Example conversation

A: I think people say four-leaf clovers are lucky because they thought they were unusual. I think people said it when they found something unusual.

B: I think the superstition came from Japan because I heard the clover with the most leaves was found in Japan.

C: I don't think people believe it. I know I don't.

Lesson 28 It must have been…

Page 68

1 Vocabulary

A

> **Answers**
>
> **Answers will vary.** Sample answer.
> I don't believe any of the news stories because I don't believe in UFOs, hairy creatures, or ghosts.

Optional Activity

Have students get into pairs and make explanations for each of the news stories.

Example conversation

A: I think the UFO was probably just a weather balloon.

B: Or it could have been a military aircraft, and the government won't admit it because it's secret.

B

Example conversation

A: I've never seen anything unusual.

B: I saw an unusual animal in the forest near my house. It was like a monkey, but monkeys don't live around here!

Optional Activity

If students haven't seen anything unusual, have them create a story.

Example conversation

A: I was driving down the road. It was late at night, and suddenly three lights went across the sky. It was amazing! It was so fast. It must have been a UFO.

2 Conversation

A

[CD 2, Track 33]

> **Answers**
>
> No, Nina doesn't think the lights were from a UFO. She thinks it couldn't have been a UFO because she doesn't believe in them.

C

[CD 2, Track 34]

> **Answers**
>
> Additional sentences underlined.
> Nina: No, I didn't. I was out of town.
> Adam: It couldn't have been birds. Birds don't have lights attached to them! And they were really big.
> Adam: Why not? How do you know?

Page 69

4 Pronunciation

A

[CD 2, Track 35]

* Tell students to remember *modal + have + verb* as a chunk of information that should be said together (i.e., blended). When students don't do this, the modal and *have* are blended, but students tend to have a pause before the verb, drawing unnatural attention to the blend.

* Tell students that *must have* is sometimes reduced to *musta* and *couldn't have* is reduced to *couldena*.

B

Example conversation

A: Someone knocked on my door and shouted my name at 3 a.m. last night.

B: You musta fallen asleep.

5 Speak with Confidence

A

Example conversation

A: I heard a voice calling my name, but no one was there.

B: You musta fallen asleep and it was a dream.

B

Example conversation

A: My partner said I musta fallen asleep and had a dream that I heard a voice calling my name.

C: It may have been a neighbor.

B: I don't think we'll be able to agree on what definitely happened.

Lessons 25 to 28 Review

English in Action

Page 70

1 Preview

> **Answers**
>
> **Answers will vary.** Sample answer.
> A "Jack of all trades, master of none" is a person who does many different things around the house, but the person doesn't do any one thing exceptionally well.

2 Practice

A

> **Answers**
>
> "Jack of all trades, master of none" is used to describe a person who can do many different things, but can't do anything extremely well.

B

> **Answers**
>
> 1. Tom
> 2. blog
> 3. shoes
> 4. Maria
> 5. teacher

Optional Questions

What does Jill write about on her blog? (She writes about customs from around the world.)

Does Jill want to be a "Jack of all trades"? (No. She wants to become really good at writing.)

3 Discuss

Example conversation

A: In my country, people should make noises when they eat noodles. Jill should blog about that.

B: That's interesting. What expression from your language do you think foreigners should know?

C: Foreigners should understand "yes" and "no" in every language they may need to use.

D: That's true, but I'd also like foreigners to know "thank you."

A: Could you explain it to me?

D: Sure…

Speak Now

Page 71

25 *Example conversation*

A: If someone invites you for dinner, you're expected to arrive at the time they say. You're not supposed to be very late, or arrive too early.

B: Right. And it's polite to bring some flowers or dessert, but you don't have to.

A: You're not supposed to bring a friend without asking the host first. They might not have enough food if someone shows up suddenly.

26 *Example conversation*

A: Do you know what *Like father, like son* means?

B: Yeah. It means that sons often act like their fathers. In other words, even though they don't try to be the same, there may be many similarities between a father and a son. What do you think *Don't put all your eggs in one basket means?*

B: I think it means don't take one chance but instead spread out your risk.

27 *Example conversation*

A: Friday the 13th is supposed to bring bad luck.

B: And the Japanese say that if you see a hearse, you should put your thumbs inside your fists, so you can't see your thumbs.

A: Really? Why?

B: If you don't, you won't be able to see your parents before they die. But no one really believes that.

28 *Example conversation*

A: A woman claims she saw a shadow in her closet. It may have been someone standing behind her.

B: It couldn't have been a stranger. It must have been her own shadow!

Lesson 29 Cars will most likely fly.

Page 72
1 Vocabulary

A

Answers
Answers will vary. Sample answer. ✓ cash   ✗ printed books   ✗ landline phones ✓ laptops   ✓ credit cards   ✗ gas-powered cars ✗ DVDs   ✗ watches   ✗ language teachers

Optional Activity

Have students brainstorm other things that may not exist in 20 years (for example, cameras, fax machines). Also have them brainstorm things that may be invented (for example, cars that drive themselves).

2 Conversation

A

[CD 2, Track 36]

Answers
The engineer said cars in the future will be faster and lighter because they will be made of a light and very strong plastic. He also said the cars will be cleaner. In the future, computers will be driving cars for humans.

B

Answers
Katie: So, could you tell me what you think cars of the future will be like? 4 Katie: Interesting. And what kind of fuels will they use? 2 Engineer: They'll likely be using hydrogen. 1 Engineer: Oh, yes…The driver will just sit back and relax. 3

Optional Activity

Have students get into pairs and talk about which predictions they agree with and why.

Page 73
3 Language Booster

B

Example conversation

A: Printed books will most likely not exist in the future.

B: Landline phones will definitely be gone.

4 Listening

A

[CD 2, Track 37]

Answers
_ **1.** (They don't predict the future. The futurologist said no one can do that.) ✓ **2.** ✓ **3.** ✓ **4.** _ **5.** (They look at the long-term future.)

Optional Activity

Have students listen again and correct the statements they did not check. (Answers above.)

B

[CD 2, Track 38]

Answers	Probable	Not probable
1.	✓	
2.	✓	
3.		✓
4.	✓	
5.		✓

Optional Activity

Have students talk about which predictions they agree with, giving reasons for their answers.

Example conversation

A: I don't think people will ever store their minds on a computer. It'd be too dangerous.

B: And medicine will probably never advance that much!

5 Speak with Confidence

B

Example conversation

A: We think there will be a cure for cancer.

B: And we also think people will start to live to be 150 years old.

C: I agree with both of your predictions.

Lesson 30 That's a really good idea!

Optional Activity

Before students open their books, ask students what global warming means. Then tell students that not all scientists agree that global warming is really happening. Ask students if they believe in global warming. Have them provide reasons for their answers.

Page 74
1 Vocabulary

A

Answers
Answers will vary. Sample answer. Students should circle things they think will change, for example: ice caps sea levels coral reefs

2 Conversation

A
[CD 2, Track 39]

Answers
Nikki thinks glass is better than plastic because plastic breaks down so slowly. Wes says it takes a lot of energy to make glass.

C
[CD 2, Track 40]

Answers
Additional sentences underlined. Nicki: That's a good idea. <u>Plastic is terrible.</u> Nicki: Because plastic breaks down so slowly. It stays on our planet for a long time. <u>It's bad for the environment.</u> Nicki: I hadn't thought of that. To be honest, I don't know what the best solution is. <u>I do think glass is prettier.</u>

Page 75
3 Language Booster

A

- Point out that we can add emphasis by using *definitely, really, much,* and *certainly*. Have students decide where to place these words within the sentence, providing the answer if necessary (before the adjectives that they modify).

- Tell students that these words make the statements stronger without changing the certainty of the statement. Contrast this with *probably* (for example, *glass is expensive* and *glass is probably more expensive*). Remind students that they must distinguish emphasis and probability.

Optional Activity

Have students brainstorm other words we can use to add emphasis (for example, absolutely, amazingly, clearly, undoubtedly). Then have them use them in sentences (for example, Glass is undoubtedly more expensive).

4 Pronunciation

A
[CD 2, Track 41]

Tell students that stressing the adverb (for example, *definitely, really, much, certainly*) has two functions. First, it can be used to make a contrast, with the speaker emphasizing the idea (for example, that the idea isn't just good but really good). Second, it can be used when providing new information.

B

Answers
Glass is **definitely** more expensive. That's a **really** good idea. Glass is **much** better than plastic. That's **certainly** bad for the environment.

5 Speak with Confidence

Remind students to practice eye contact while talking.

Lesson 31 I'll pick you up.

Page 76

1 Vocabulary

A

Answers	
2. the counter	**6.** the garbage
3. the pencils	**7.** my children
4. the dishes	**8.** the counter
5. the yard	

Optional Activity

Have students think of two-word verbs to use with the words they crossed out. To increase the challenge, encourage them to think of combinations not already used in Part 1. (For example, *wipe off the counter* is used in number 6, so they should think of another verb to use with counter.)

Answers	
Answers will vary. Sample answer.	
1. clean up the building	**5.** clean up the yard
2. dry off the counter	**6.** throw out the garbage
3. hand out the pencils	**7.** drop off my children
4. pile up the dishes	**8.** clean off the counter

B

Example conversation

A: I never put away the groceries because I don't do the grocery shopping. But I always hang up my clothes.

B: I often clean out my desk. If I don't, I can't get my work done.

2 Conversation

A

[CD 2, Track 42]

Answers
Dan and Mike are having a goodbye party because Mike is leaving for the summer.
Doug is going to drive Carlos to the party.

Ask students what *pick you up* means, providing the answer if necessary. (It means to go to someone's location and giving them a ride in your car to another place. It does not mean physically lifting someone.)

C

[CD 2, Track 43]

Answers
Additional sentences underlined.
Doug: Yeah. So, can you make it? <u>Please say yes.</u>
Carlos: Sure. I'll hurry and get all this stuff done. <u>It won't take long.</u>
Doug: OK. I'll come around 7 p.m. <u>I'll call when I'm there.</u>

Page 77

3 Language Booster

Tell students that we often also use *on* when describing plans. For example, *I plan on going to Mexico this summer* or *I'm planning on giving a speech at the conference.* Note that we don't use *on* with the expressions *I'm going to…* or *I have to…*

4 Pronunciation

A

[CD 2, Track 44]

Tell students we stress both words when the verb is the focus of the sentence. Explain that the verb is usually new information.

5 Speak with Confidence

A

Answers
Answers will vary. Sample answer.
1. clean up my room
2. pick up the living room
3. drop off the dry-cleaning
4. pick up the dry-cleaning
5. take out the garbage
6. put away the dishes

Lesson 32 What do you hope to do?

Page 78

1 Vocabulary

A

Answers
Answers will vary. Sample answer.

9 be financially independent	4 go to graduate school
2 lose weight	6 move out of my parents' home
3 be more confident	1 manage money better
8 get out of debt	5 get in better shape
7 get my own place	

B

Example conversation

A: I think it's going to be really hard to be financially independent.

B: I agree. It will be easier to manage my money better. I just have to be more careful.

A: But that will still be hard.

2 Conversation

A

[CD 2, Track 45]

Answers
Hung doesn't want to get a job right after graduation. He wants to travel around Europe. Nicole wants to get a job right away. Then she hopes to move out of her parents' home and get her own place.

B

Answers
Nicole: So, do you have any plans after graduation? 1 Hung: I don't want to get a job right away…I'd like to take some time off and travel around Europe. 4 Hung: I'm not sure…I don't know if I can go to all three. 2 Hung: I wish I could get my own place, too. 3

Page 79

3 Language Booster

A

Point out that students shouldn't use *to* with *could*. Tell students that sentences with *could* express a wish that the speaker thinks may not come true in the near future. The meaning is *I wish I could …, but…*

4 Listening

A

[CD 2, Track 46]

Answers	
a. 2	**c.** 4
b. 1	**d.** 3

Optional Activity

Have students say what each speaker's goals are.

Answers
1. be more confident and be able to give presentations at sales meetings
2. be in better shape
3. manage money better
4. be financially independent

B

[CD 2, Track 46]

Answers
1. by taking a public speaking class
2. by jogging with friends
3. by taking an online class
4. by having a coach help him

C

Example conversation

A: I want to get in shape, but I don't like running or jogging. I could start walking, maybe.

B: I'd like to manage my money better. I think I should keep track of how I spend my money for a month and then look for ways to spend less.

5 Speak with Confidence

A

Answers
Answers will vary. Sample answer. Within the next year: get in shape Within the next few years: get a new job Within the next ten years: be financially independent

Lessons 29 to 32 Review

English in Action

Page 80

1 Preview

> **Answers**
>
> **Answers will vary.** Sample answer.
> a. This picture is of friends spending time together. I think it might represent our future.
> b. This picture shows a person watching many different TV screens at the same time. I think that represents the future.
> c. This is a picture of a city in the future. It may represent the future.
> d. This car can grow a plant. It gives us oxygen and reduces carbon dioxide. I don't think that really represents the future.

2 Practice

> **Answers**
>
> 1. Maria   3. Jill
> 2. Eric   4. Tom

Optional Questions

What are Tom's goals for the future? (Tom wants to have a family. He also wants a job that will let him travel a lot.)

What is Eric's hope for the future? (He hopes he finds the cure for cancer.)

What is Maria's dream for the future? (She wants to have her own place and be financially independent.)

What is Jill's goal? (She wants millions of visitors to log on to her website.)

3 Discuss

Example conversation

A: I think none of them are very likely to happen.

B: Well, out of the four, I guess number 2 is the most likely. But what about inventions? What is one invention you hope we will have in the future?

C: I hope to have a robot that does all the cooking, cleaning, shopping, and washing.

D: What will you do?

C: Work, have fun with friends, and see the world!

Speak Now

Page 81

29 *Example conversation*

A: In the future, space travel could be possible.

B: Mobile phones will probably be part of our clothes so we won't have to worry about forgetting them.

A: In the future, cars will definitely use less gas, but I don't think they'll use hydrogen. With less gas, our cities will be cleaner.

30 *Example conversation*

A: Pollution is definitely something we need to try to reduce.

B: I agree. We can't keep ignoring all of the problems that are caused by pollution.

A: Climate change is certainly getting worse.

B: I'm not so sure. Even the scientists can't agree.

31 *Example conversation*

A: Tonight I'm going to go to dinner with Marc and Steven.

B: Cool! I plan to go to a movie with Craig and Chris. Do you guys want to come with us?

A: Sounds great. We're eating at Panda World.

B: That's right by my house. I'll pick you guys up at 8:30 and we can go to the theater. Craig and Chris are meeting me at 8:45.

A: Sounds great. See you then.

32 *Example conversation*

B: What are your goals for the future?

A: I want to get a job as a pilot.

B: Isn't that hard?

A: Yeah, but I'm going to flight school now. And I'll graduate with a degree in Aviation. That will help.

B: Do you have to learn another language?

A: No. In many countries, English is the language for aviation.

1 I'm an only child.

Part 1

Match the words on the left with their definitions on the right.

1. single   **A.** A person who doesn't have any siblings

2. engaged   **B.** A person who is not married

3. divorced   **C.** A person who is the oldest child in a family

4. fiancé (m.) / fiancée (fem.)   **D.** A person who was married but isn't any more

5. spouse   **E.** A person who has an older brother and a younger sister

6. middle child   **F.** A person who has promised to get married

7. firstborn   **G.** The person you are married to

8. only child   **H.** The person you are going to marry

Part 2

Complete each conversation using the words and phrases in Part 1. In class, practice the conversations with a partner.

1.

Yumi: Hi, Matt. The other day I saw someone who looks a lot like you. Do you have a sister who is about 20 years old?

Matt: No. In fact, I don't have any brothers and sisters. I'm _____.

2.

Patricia: I heard you are getting married. Congratulations!

Dolores: Thanks. Now that I am _____, there is so much to do to plan the wedding.

3.

Frank: I don't think I'll ever get married.

Anders: Really? You want to be _____ your whole life? Not me! I want to have a _____, some kids, and a nice little house.

Frank: You're crazy!

4.

Marco: Didn't you tell me you have a lot of brothers and sisters?

Paula: Yeah. I have three brothers and two sisters. I'm the oldest so I always help my mom.

Marco: Oh, so you're the _____. That must be fun but also a little hard.

Paula: Yeah, but I love my brothers and sisters. It's always crazy at my house, but always fun.

2 She's a born leader.

Part 1

Are these words positive, negative, or both? Write them in the diagram. In class, talk about your ideas with a partner.

a role model   a follower   a loner   a pessimist   a know-it-all   an optimist
a born leader   a problem solver

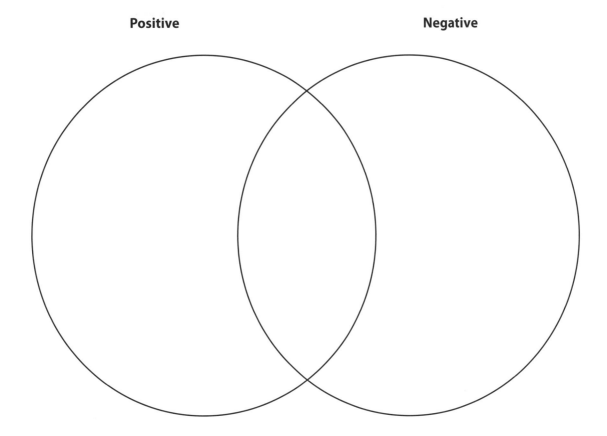

Positive　　　　　　　　　　　　**Negative**

Part 2

Complete the sentences with ideas from Part 1 and your own ideas. Make sentences that are true for you. In class, take turns reading your sentences with a partner.

1. _____ is a born leader.

2. A _____ should also be _____.

3. I'm a _____.

4. I don't really like people who are _____.

5. _____ is an optimist, but _____ is a pessimist.

6. A good role model must _____.

7. A problem solver _____.

8. _____ should be class president. He/She is a(n) _____.

9. Followers are often _____.

3 We're both reliable.

Part 1

Unscramble the characteristics of people.

1. _____ doyom
2. _____ ilbaelre
3. _____ iedosnrecta
4. _____ taerum

5. _____ belxefil
6. _____ teamumir
7. _____ ivggriofn
8. _____ eresbilnops

Part 2

Use the words from Part 1 to complete each sentence. In class, take turns reading the sentences with a partner.

1. Whenever you have a problem, your uncle is always there for you. He is very _____.

2. Even though he is only 18 years old, he is in his third year at university. He is very _____ for his age.

3. You like to change your plans a lot, but luckily your friend is _____ and doesn't get upset.

4. When your brother does something wrong, your mother doesn't stay angry very long. She is _____.

5. Movie stars who are angry one minute but kind the next become famous because they are _____.

6. She's 20 years old, but she acts like she is 15. She's _____.

7. People know you will take care of things in your classroom. They think you are _____.

8. Your friend always thinks about other people and how they feel. She is _____.

Part 3

Use the words from Part 1 to write the opposites.

1. irresponsible _____
2. immature _____
3. unforgiving _____

4. inflexible _____
5. inconsiderate _____
6. unreliable _____

In class, use the opposites with a partner.

A: My sister is a little irresponsible. Yesterday, she didn't call to tell my mom that she would be late for dinner. My mom was worried.

B: So your sister needs to be more _____.

A: Yeah.

4 As I was saying…

Read the conversations. What values are they talking about? Write your answer on the line. In class, talk about why you chose the values. Then practice the conversations with a partner.

1. _____

A: I don't understand this homework at all!

B: Don't worry. I'll help you.

2. _____

Mom: It's important to help your friends when they need it. And not to gossip about them. And if someone says something bad about them, you shouldn't agree.

Son: I know, Mom. You tell me all the time!

3. _____

A: Mateo always uses Mr. and Mrs. when he is talking with people he just met.

B: And he never interrupts.

4. _____

A: Collin never tells a lie.

B: Yeah, and at a store, if someone gives him too much money, he never keeps it.

5. _____

A: Last night Mr. Sher stayed at school to help me until 8:00.

B: He's really great. He always gives students help, even when he needs to do other things.

6. _____ and _____

Radio announcer: Last night, there was a big fire on Main and First. Before the firefighters got there, some neighbors went into the house and helped the people. We have a caller who was there.

Caller: It was amazing. The fire was everywhere. But the neighbors went in, even though it was really dangerous.

7. _____

A: Massimo doesn't give up. If he can't do something, he keeps practicing until he can.

B: I know. I saw him practicing basketball for four hours last Saturday!

8. _____

News reporter 1: And now, a fantastic story! Last night, there was a big car accident.

News reporter 2: That's right, Bob. Two cars drove by without doing anything. But then a man stopped to help, and because of him, no one died.

News reporter 1: He reminds us that it is important to help others.

9. _____ and _____

A: That team is famous because when they win, they are really kind to the other team.

B: And when they lose, they are kind, too.

5 I'd like to check in.

Part 1

Rank these places to stay from a (most expensive) to e (least expensive). Then write two words or phrases that describe the good points of each place.

1. _____ dorm _____ *convenient location, meet new people* _____

2. _____ hotel _____

3. _____ motel _____

4. _____ campground _____

5. _____ youth hostel _____

In class, compare answers with a partner. Did you rank the places to stay in the same order?

A: We can meet new people in dorms.

B: Yeah, and they are very convenient.

Part 2

What do the places in Part 1 usually have? Write the places in the diagram. In class, compare answers with a partner.

Business center   **Pool**   **Neither**

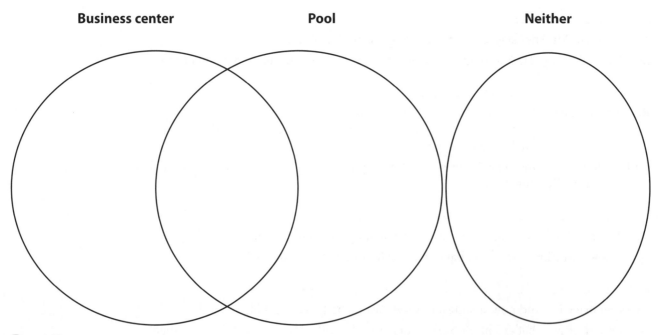

Part 3

Answer the questions so they are true for you. In class, take turns asking and answering the questions with a partner.

1. Do you prefer to stay in a single or double when you travel? Why?

_____

2. Is it better to make a reservation or get a place to stay when you get to the city? Why?

_____

6 Here are some rules.

Part 1

Match the words on the left with their meanings on the right.

1.	curfew	A.	sound(s)
2.	key	B.	the place where you exercise
3.	noise	C.	people who belong to a group
4.	pool	D.	ordering food and drinks that are brought to your room
5.	guests	E.	the time by which you must return to the place you are staying
6.	bathroom	F.	expensive or important things
7.	health club	G.	the place where you take a shower or bath
8.	valuables	H.	the place where you swim
9.	members	I.	the people staying at a hotel
10.	room service	J.	the thing you use to unlock a door

Part 2

Imagine you are the manager of a new hotel and must decide what is allowed and not allowed. Write the rules for each topic in Part 1. You can also make suggestions instead of rules. (Please…) In class, compare answers with a partner.

1. _____ There is no curfew. You can stay out as late as you want. _____
2. _____
3. _____
4. _____
5. _____
6. _____
7. _____
8. _____
9. _____
10. _____

7 There are some problems.

Part 1

Where do you find these things? Write the words in the diagram below. Add at least one thing to each place. In class, compare answers with a partner.

TV   sink   shower   closet   toilet   lamp   desk   bed

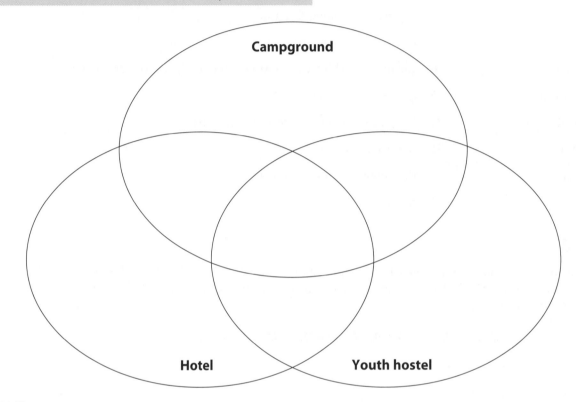

Part 2

Write the problems with a hotel room. In class, practice the conversations with a partner.

1.

A: _____ .

B: I'm very sorry. I'll have someone bring you a new remote so you can change the channels.

2.

A: _____ .

B: I can ask housekeeping to bring you some clean pillows right away.

3.

A: _____ .

B: I'll have a plumber come and look at it.

4.

A: _____ .

B: Let me get someone to come and clean it.

8 That would be great.

Part 1

Would you like to do these jobs? Rank them from 1 (want to be the most) to 8 (want to be the least).

_____ a restaurant server   _____ a train reservations agent

_____ a flight attendant   _____ a travel agent

_____ a salesclerk   _____ a hotel clerk

_____ a bus driver   _____ a parking attendant

In class, compare answers with a partner. When you can, give reasons for your answers.

A: I'd like to be a travel agent the most.

B: Really? Why?

A: I know a lot about different cities and I like helping people.

Part 2

In each conversation, there is a mistake. Cross it out and write the correct word(s) on the line. In class, practice the correct conversations with your partner.

1. **A:** I can tell you when we're at the stop for the mall.

   B: That ~~could~~ be great. Thanks.
   _____ **would** _____

2. **A:** I be happy to order a size 10 for you. It'd be here in a week.

   B: That won't be necessary. _____

3. **A:** Do you like me to give you a minute to look at the menu?

   B: That's OK. _____

4. **A:** Would you want me to purchase your plane ticket for you?

   B: Yes, thank you. _____

5. **A:** Something to drink?

   B: No. I'd like a cola, please. Oh, and when are we going to be landing? _____

6. **A:** I can give you a double instead of a single.

   B: Really? I'd appreciating that.
   _____

Part 3

In each conversation in Part 2, what is A's job? Write the jobs listed in Part 1 on each line.

1. _____

2. _____

3. _____

4. _____

5. _____

6. _____

Lesson 8   **49**

9 Do you know…?

Part 1

How often do you go to these places? Put the places into the best column for you. In class, talk about your ideas with a partner.

| health food store | hair salon | food court | electronics store | office supply store |
| travel agency | boutique | dry cleaners | | |

More than once a month	Once a month	Few times a year/Never
_____	_____	_____
_____	_____	_____
_____	_____	_____
_____	_____	_____
_____	_____	_____
_____	_____	_____
_____	_____	_____
_____	_____	_____

Part 2

Complete the conversations with true information about your city. In class, practice the conversations with a partner.

1.

Lester: Can you tell me where a good food court is?

You: _____.

2.

Eric: Do you know how much the haircuts are around here?

You: _____.

3.

Leah: Do you know if I can use a credit card at the dry cleaners?

You: _____.

4.

Renee: Can you tell me where I can buy health food?

You: _____.

5.

Gus: Can you tell me if there's a travel agency near here?

You: _____.

10 Sorry. My mistake.

Read the hints and write the words to complete the crossword puzzle.

Across

1. When a salesclerk told you to pay less than the real price, you were _____.
3. The money you get back because you paid more than the price.
5. When the letters in a word are not correct or in the wrong order.
6. When you can't find something, it's _____.

Down

2. A piece of paper you get after you buy something that shows what you paid.
4. When a salesclerk asked you to pay more than the real price, you were _____.

11 Can I please…?

Part 1

Read the conversations. What job are they talking about? Write your answer on the line. In class, practice the conversations with a partner.

1. _____

A: My dog isn't eating. Can I make an appointment?

B: What time are you free?

2. _____

A: I'm here for a haircut.

B: OK. Who is your appointment with?

3. _____

A: I want lots of flowers and a huge cake. My fiancé wants to have a dance after the dinner.

B: It will be a day you will never forget!

4. _____

A: You need to know a lot about food and you have to be creative. If you are interested, you should talk to some chefs and see if this would be a good job for you.

B: Can you tell me how to set up an appointment with a chef?

5. _____

A: You still haven't taken a foreign language. You must take at least one year of French, German, Chinese, or Korean before you finish school.

B: I know. I'm going to take Chinese next year.

6. _____

Mom: Let's have some photos taken of the family. The kids are growing so fast.

Dad: OK. I'll make an appointment. How about next Saturday?

7. _____

A: Taku is great. Even when I couldn't get it to turn on, he got all my files off the hard drive.

B: Can you call him and make an appointment for me?

8. _____

A: I've had a sore throat for three days.

B: You better make an appointment today. You know how busy his office gets.

12 I'm broke.

Part 1

Write the problem that matches the complaint.

1. I can't remember anything. _____

2. I don't have any money! _____ _____

3. I feel like I have too many things to do. How can I get them all done? _____

4. I'm worried about everything. _____

5. I can't stay awake. _____

6. I feel sad all the time. _____

7. I feel like I'm all alone. _____

8. I have the flu. _____

Part 2

Choose five of the problems from Part 1. For each conversation, write a recommendation (what A says). Acknowledge the recommendation (what B says). Use a different acknowledgement for each. In class, take turns reading your conversations with a partner. Can your partner guess which problem you are talking about?

1.

A: _____ .

B: _____ .

2.

A: _____ .

B: _____ .

3.

A: _____ .

B: _____ .

4.

A: _____ .

B: _____ .

5.

A: _____ .

B: _____ .

13 I used to play hopscotch.

Part 1

In the puzzle below, find the six words from childhood. The words go

P	G	Z	U	W	D	T	G	H	T	I	H	A
B	L	H	H	T	S	E	A	D	C	A	B	H
O	B	A	A	O	Y	O	R	G	H	O	G	S
J	U	C	Y	A	O	R	E	U	E	R	E	S
B	P	M	T	G	Y	D	E	J	C	N	I	M
O	N	O	B	E	R	L	Y	E	K	E	L	L
I	R	L	M	D	A	O	N	L	E	G	B	B
M	E	O	L	T	B	U	U	U	R	H	I	K
T	J	I	G	M	Y	R	B	N	S	T	C	O
S	H	Y	O	U	R	U	A	G	D	R	C	R
C	C	T	G	U	L	L	H	O	L	H	I	O
Q	D	L	W	L	O	E	M	D	E	O	K	H
F	A	N	Y	H	O	P	S	C	O	T	C	H
O	P	I	N	O	Z	Z	O	P	D	U	L	N

Part 2

Look at the letters you didn't circle. Write every 4th letter below to find the hidden question. Write your answer on the line. Take turns asking and answering the question with a partner in class.

 W   H _____ _____   _____ _____   _____ _____ _____ _____

_____ _____ _____ _____ _____ _____ _____ _____ _____

_____ _____ _____ _____ _____   _____ _____ _____ _____

_____ _____ _____ _____ _____ _____ _____ _____ _____ ?

Answer: _____

14 She said she was sorry.

Part 1

Are these words positive, negative, or both? Write them in the diagram. In class, talk about your ideas with a partner.

lucky   strange   awful   embarrassing   scary   disgusting   romantic

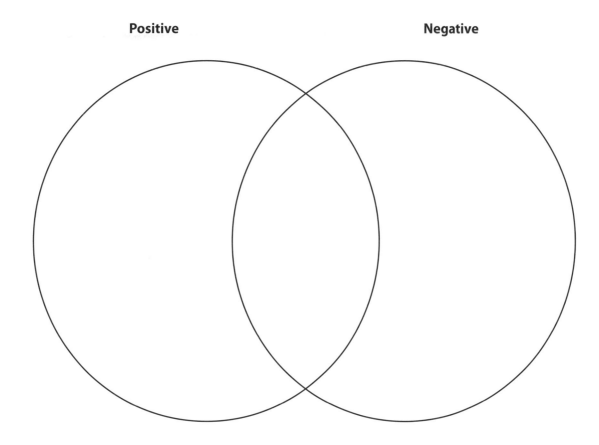

Positive   **Negative**

Part 2

In each conversation, there is one mistake. Cross it out and write the correct word(s) on the line. In class, practice the correct conversations with your partner.

1. **A:** How embarrassing!

   B: Yeah. But then she says she was sorry.

   _____

2. **A:** I said I would help her, but she said, "Forget it."

   B: What awful! _____

3. **A:** Mom said she hasn't been there since last week.

   B: What? I thought she went yesterday.

   _____

4. **A:** I said I will ask her for an autograph. Why are you asking me again?

   B: Because I don't want you to forget!

   _____

5. **A:** Bob went to Casual Dining last week.

   B: Yeah. He told to me that they had good food.

   _____

6. **A:** What happened then?

   B: Well, Matthew said he love her, and Maria said, "Why?" _____

15 I read an unusual story.

Part 1

Choose the best word or phrase to complete each news headline.

1. School (cancels / denies) lunch program.

2. Richest man in the world (catches / donates) $1,000,000.

3. Money (saves / scores) the school lunch program.

4. President (closes / catches) flu, cancels trip.

5. Super Bowl XLVI (breaks / saves) record as most-watched TV program in history!

6. Popular restaurant (closes / crashes) because of bad economy.

7. Winter storm (causes / cancels) schools closings.

8. New plane (crashes / breaks), killing three.

9. Musician (denies / donates) rumors about new album.

10. Freese (scores /causes) the winning run in game six of the World Series!

Part 2

Which word is different? Circle it. In class, with a partner talk about why it is different.

1. (drop)	catch	get
2. touch	crash	hit
3. cause	allow	make
4. hurt	break	fix
5. accept	deny	refuse
6. stop	change	cancel
7. score	get	miss
8. donate	give	take
9. rescue	save	find

Part 3

Answer the questions. In class, compare answers with a partner.

1. Have you ever donated anything? _____.

   What? _____.

2. What do people try not to crash? Give three ideas. _____.

16 When did they release it?

Part 1

How important are these things to your life? Rank them from 1 (the most important) to 8 (the least important). Then write one example of each. In class, compare answers with a partner.

_____ a natural disaster   _____ *earthquakes* _____

_____ a political change   _____

_____ a sporting success   _____

_____ a key discovery   _____

_____ a royal wedding   _____

_____ a celebrity scandal   _____

_____ a daring rescue   _____

Part 2

Use the topics from Part 1. Write questions and complete the answers. In class, practice the conversations with a partner.

1.

A: _____ Olympics?

B: They were in _____.

2.

A: _____?

B: The _____ wedding was on _____ 29 in _____.

3.

A: _____?

B: _____ hosted _____ in _____.

4.

A: _____?

B: _____ was elected _____ 4 in _____.

5.

A: _____?

B: _____ became _____ in _____.

17 You didn't know?

Part 1

Who do you talk with about these topics? Write the types of friends in the diagram. In class, get together with a partner and talk about why you put each one where you did.

> an old friend   an acquaintance   a best friend   a former friend   a lifelong friend
> a childhood friend   a fair-weather friend

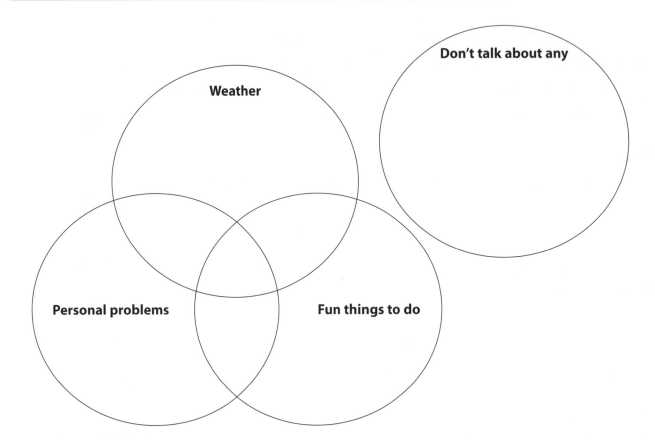

Part 2

For each conversation, complete A's comment and then write B's reaction by using a reply question. In class, practice the conversations with a partner.

1.

A: My best friend _____.

B: _____.

2.

A: The other day I ran into a childhood friend and _____.

B: _____.

3.

A: _____ is a lifelong friend, but _____.

B: _____.

18 A good friend is loyal.

Part 1

What's important in a colleague? Rank these characteristics from 1 (the most important) to 7 (less important). When colleagues don't have these characteristics, which cause the most problems? On the second line, rank them from *a* (causes the biggest problems) to *g* (cause the least problems). If you don't know, guess. In class, talk about your ideas with a partner.

_____ accepting   _____

_____ reliable   _____

_____ forgiving   _____

_____ truthful   _____

_____ loyal   _____

_____ supportive   _____

_____ caring   _____

Part 2

Use your ideas from Part 1 to complete the conversation. In class, practice the conversation with a partner.

A: What's important to you in a colleague?

B: The most important thing is how _____ someone is.
(1)

A: To me, a colleague needs to be _____. I think being _____ is
(2)   (3)
less important.

B: Why? Don't you think that's important, too?

A: _____.
(4)

B: Interesting. To me _____, too.
(5)

A: What do you think causes the most problems at work?

B: I think the most problems are caused by not being _____ and _____.
(6)   (6)

A: Yeah, but _____.
(7)

B: What about for your boss?

A: It's important for a boss to be _____.
(8)

B: Yeah, but _____.
(9)

A: I know what you mean.

Lesson 18   **59**

19 I could do that.

Part 1

Rank these ways of making new friends from 1 (the easiest for you) to 9 (the most difficult for you). On the second line write a reason. In class, compare answers with a partner and talk about your reasons.

——— take a class ————————————————————————————

——— join a student club ————————————————————————

——— make friends through friends ———————————————————

——— introduce yourself to people ————————————————————

——— join an online group —————————————————————————

——— go to social events ——————————————————————————

——— use social networks ——————————————————————————

——— play sports ——————————————————————————————

——— do volunteer work ————————————————————————————

Part 2

Use your ideas from Part 1 and other ideas to complete the conversation. Partner 1 should comment positively but Partner 2 should comment negatively each time but the last time. In class, get into groups of three and practice the conversation.

You: 1. If you want to make new friends, the best thing to do is ————————————.

Partner 1:   2. ————————————————————————————————.

Partner 2:   3. ————————————————————————————————.

You: 4. Well, another good idea is ————————————————————.

Partner 1:   Why?

You: 5. Because ————————————————————————————————.

Partner 1:   6. ————————————————————————————————.

Partner 2:   7. ————————————————————————————————.

You: What do you suggest?

Partner 2:   8. ————————————————————————————————.

20 I wish I'd remembered.

Part 1

Write the words from the box to complete the definitions.

ignored   involve   joke   problems   feelings   apologize

1. Anger, love, sadness, and happiness are examples of _____

2. Someone _____ you when they acted like they didn't see or hear you.

3. To say you are sorry is to _____.

4. Situations that are not easy are _____.

5. To include someone in something is to _____ them.

6. When you say something to make people laugh you tell a _____.

Part 2

Use the words from Part 1 to complete the story.

Even if you are lifelong friends, people have _____ in their relationships once in
a while. I'll give you an example. My friend is a little moody. Recently, even though he saw me, he
_____ me. Later, when I asked him about it, he made a _____
and said I shouldn't be so serious about everything. He didn't _____. I guess
he didn't think he did anything wrong. That makes me wonder. "Doesn't he know he hurt my
_____?" I don't want to _____ our other friends, but I want to
find a good solution. What do you suggest?

With a partner talk about the question and offer solutions.

A: Something she might try is telling the friend how she feels.
B: What she could do is ignore the friend, and see how he feels.

Part 3

Complete the sentences. In class, talk about your ideas with a partner.

1. I wish I had remembered _____.

2. I wish I hadn't forgotten about _____.

   I should have put a reminder _____.

3. I wish _____.

21 I'd rather not say.

Part 1

Are these things you can learn for free or are they sometimes but not always free? Write them in the diagram. In class, talk about your ideas with a partner. Give reasons for your ideas.

leadership   computer skills   work experience   overseas experience   good school grades
a graduate degree   communication skills   knowledge of current affairs   fluency in English

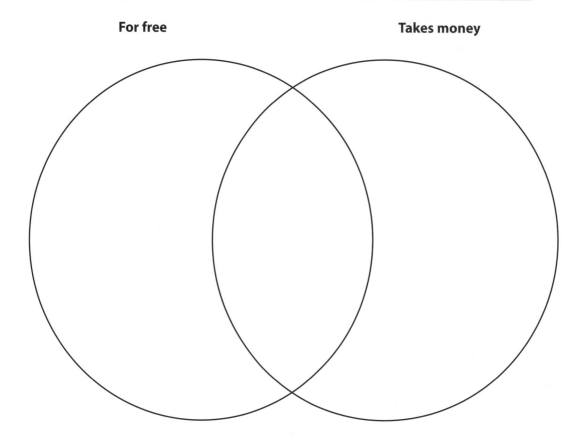

For free   **Takes money**

Part 2

Which of the things in Part 1 do you have now?

_____

Which of the things in Part 1 do you want, or want more of?

_____

In class, compare answers with a partner. Talk about how you can get those skills without spending too much money.

A: I want more communication skills.

B: I do, too.

A: We could join a speech club. They take turns giving speeches and help each other get better.

B: That's a good idea. We could also watch speeches by famous people and learn what they did.

22 It could be an ad for…

Part 1

How often do you pay for these products and services? Rank them from 1 (most often) to 7 (least often/never). On the second line, write two or three ideas about how companies try to sell these things. In class, compare answers with a partner.

_____ fast food _____ *easy, saves time, cheap* _____

_____ online travel service _____

_____ soft drinks _____

_____ office supplies _____

_____ bus line _____

_____ amusement park _____

_____ hair coloring _____

Part 2

What do you think about each of the things in Part 1? Put them in the diagram. In class, with your partner talk about why you put each one where you did.

Something necessary　　　　**Something fun**

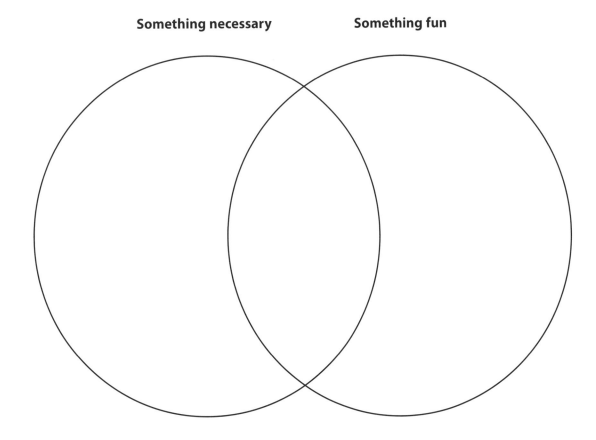

23 The main reason is...

Part 1

Write the business that matches the definition.

| shopping mall   bank   convenience store   language school   supermarket   airline |

1. _____ a place to learn how to speak a different language

2. _____ a company that flies people from one place to another

3. _____ a place to buy food

4. _____ a place that is open all day and night and has lots of drinks and snacks

5. _____ a place that has one or more buildings with many different stores

6. _____ a place to keep money

Part 2

Which businesses in Part 1 are becoming popular on the Internet?

_____

Which businesses could be replaced by companies on the Internet?

_____

In class, talk about your ideas with your partner. Give reasons for your answers.

A: Airlines can't be replaced by the Internet.

B: That's true, but we can buy tickets on the Internet instead of going to a travel agent.

Part 3

Answer the questions. In class, take turns asking and answering the questions with a partner. Ask follow-up questions so your partner gives reasons for each answer.

1. How often do you go to shopping malls? _____.

2. Do you use online banks? _____.

3. How often do you go to convenience stores? _____.

4. Have you ever gone to a language school? _____.

5. Where is the nearest supermarket? _____.

6. What are three things you can buy at a supermarket that you can't buy at a convenience store?

_____

7. What is the most popular airline in your country? _____.

24 It needs a good location.

Part 1

When you think about going to a new store, what do you think about the most? Rank these things from 1 (the most important) to 6 (the least important). In class, talk about your ideas with a partner.

service   idea   location   marketing   prices   logo

_____   _____

_____   _____

_____   _____

Part 2

Read the conversations. What topics from Part 1 are they talking about? Write your answer on the line. In class, practice the conversations with a partner.

1. _____

A: What's the most famous one in the world?

B: Maybe the yellow M on the red background for that fast food restaurant.

2. _____

A: I stayed at that new hotel the other day, but I won't stay again. It's so far from everything.

B: Oh really?

3. _____

A: This flyer was on my car.

B: It looks like there's a new restaurant in the area. That's a good way to tell people about it.

4. _____

A: Have you been to that new Thai restaurant yet?

B: Yeah, it's reasonable, and the food is fantastic!

5. _____

A: That hotel is just like every other one.

B: I agree. They need to think of something different. You don't know if you are in New York or Paris or Beijing!

6. _____

A: The manager was very helpful.

B: And the housekeeper gave me more towels without asking. I'd definitely go back there again.

25 You're expected to...

Part 1

Unscramble each of the verbs about expectations.

1. _____ enilcde

2. _____ owb

3. _____ wconegkeald

4. _____ kaehs

5. _____ uopr

6. _____ cpecat

7. _____ cdeepxet

Part 2

Imagine a foreigner is going to visit your country. What should he or she know? Use the words from Part 1 and the topics below to give the foreigner help. In class, compare answers with a partner.

1. eating _____

2. meeting people _____

3. greetings _____

4. drinking _____

5. at parties _____

6. entering homes _____

7. visiting someone _____

8. meeting for the first time _____

9. going out _____

10. teachers _____

11. going to hospitals _____

12. talking to teachers _____

Part 3

Think about your answers in Part 2. How many times did you and your partner have the same advice? _____

How many times did you have different advice? _____ Talk about why with your partner.

© Oxford University Press. Permission granted to reproduce for classroom use.

Put the words into the correct place in the puzzle. Then write a clue for each word. In class, compare answers with a partner.

| variety | charity | knowledge | haste | diligence | ignorance | virtue |

Across

2. _____   6. _____

Down

1. _____   4. _____

2. _____   5. _____

3. _____

27 What will happen if…?

Part 1

In the puzzle below, find the six words about superstitions. The words go

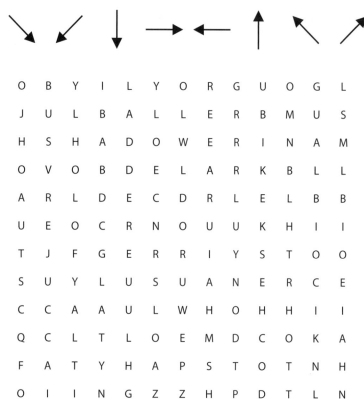

O	B	Y	I	L	Y	O	R	G	U	O	G	L
J	U	L	B	A	L	L	E	R	B	M	U	S
H	S	H	A	D	O	W	E	R	I	N	A	M
O	V	O	B	D	E	L	A	R	K	B	L	L
A	R	L	D	E	C	D	R	L	E	L	B	B
U	E	O	C	R	N	O	U	U	K	H	I	I
T	J	F	G	E	R	R	I	Y	S	T	O	O
S	U	Y	L	U	S	U	A	N	E	R	C	E
C	C	A	A	U	L	W	H	O	H	H	I	I
Q	C	L	T	L	O	E	M	D	C	O	K	A
F	A	T	Y	H	A	P	S	T	O	T	N	H
O	I	I	N	G	Z	Z	H	P	D	T	L	N

Part 2

Look at the letters you didn't circle. Write every 3rd letter below to find the hidden message.

__Y__ _____ _____ _____ _____   _____ _____ _____ _____

_____ _____ _____ _____   _____ _____ _____ _____   _____ _____

_____ _____ _____ _____   _____ _____ _____ _____   _____ _____

_____ _____ _____ _____ _____   _____ _____ _____ _____

_____ _____   _____ _____ _____ _____ _____ _____.

Do you agree? Why or why not? _____
In class, talk about your answers with your partner.

28 It must have been…

Part 1

Put the words into the correct place in the puzzle.

| ghost | creature | bear | fake | smoke | UFO | aliens | aircraft | balloon | reflection | gorilla | costume |

Part 2

Write a clue for each word. In class, compare answers with a partner.

Across

2. _____
4. _____
5. _____
6. _____

7. _____
9. _____
10. _____

Down

1. _____
2. _____
3. _____

5. _____
8. _____

Lesson 28   **69**

29 Cars will most likely fly.

Part 1

How often do you use or see these things? Put them into the best column for you. In class, talk about your ideas with a partner.

| cash | printed books | landline phones | laptops | credit cards |
| DVDs | watches | language teachers | gas-powered cars | |

All the time	**Sometimes**	**Never**
_____	_____	_____
_____	_____	_____
_____	_____	_____
_____	_____	_____
_____	_____	_____
_____	_____	_____
_____	_____	_____
_____	_____	_____

Part 2

In each conversation, there is a mistake. Cross it out and write the correct word(s) on the line. In class, practice the correct conversations with your partner.

1. **A:** We probably won't drive anymore.

   B: Yeah. Cars will all likely drive themselves.

   _____

2. **A:** In the future, people may definitely live on the moon.

   B: I'm not sure about that.

   _____

3. **A:** Planes will use power from the sun.

   B: And it's like that cars will, too.

   _____

4. **A:** Computers would cook for us.

   B: Wouldn't that be great?

   _____

5. **A:** Humans may probably go to Mars.

   B: But it will be a long trip.

   _____

6. **A:** Robots would look just like humans.

   B: Do you really think so?

   _____

Part 3

Look at the conversations in Part 2. Is A making a probable (P) or definite (D) prediction?

1. _____
2. _____
3. _____
4. _____
5. _____
6. _____

30 That's a really good idea!

Part 1

Unscramble the things that may be affected by climate change. On the second line, rank the problems from a (most serious) to h (least serious). In class, talk about your ideas with a partner.

1. _____ _____ iecspac _____
2. _____ _____ ciesaenimslap _____
3. _____ iicste _____
4. _____ snifaroetrs _____
5. _____ _____ errhstawfe _____
6. _____ ostmrs _____
7. _____ _____ eslavelse _____
8. _____ _____ reosfacrle _____

Part 2

If the climate changes, what will be affected? Put the words from Part 1 in the diagram. In class, with your partner talk about why you put each one where you did.

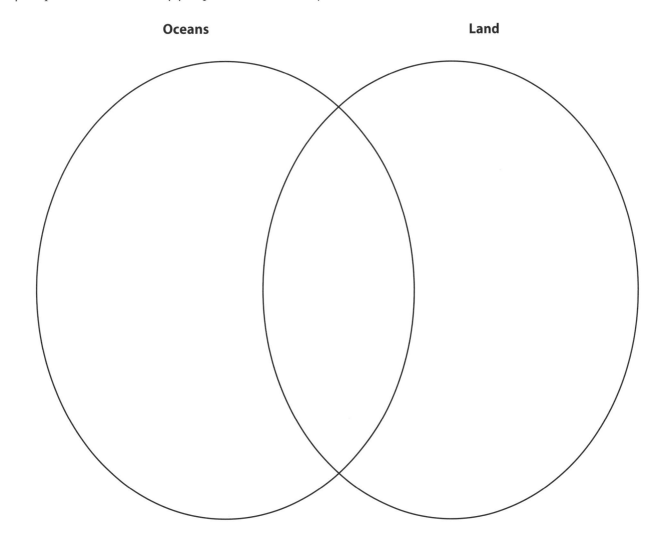

Oceans　　　　　　　　　**Land**

31 I'll pick you up.

Part 1

Use the words in the box to complete each chore. If a word is not needed, write an X. On the second line, write two words or phrases about your chores. In class, compare your ideas with a partner.

| out   away   up   off |

1. pick _____ _____*groceries, the room*_____

2. clean _____ _____

3. throw _____ _____

4. put _____ _____

5. take _____ _____

6. wipe _____ _____

7. drop _____ _____

8. hang _____ _____

Part 2

How often do you do the chores in Part 1? Put them into the best column for you. In class, talk about your ideas with a partner.

Every day	Several times a week	Never
_____	*pick up the room*	_____
_____	_____	_____
_____	_____	_____
_____	_____	_____
_____	_____	_____
_____	_____	_____

Part 3

Complete the conversation with your ideas in Part 1. In class, practice the conversations with a partner.

A: I really don't like to _____.
(1)

B: I know what you mean, but it isn't fun to _____, either.
(2)

A: That's true. It's easy to _____, though.
(3)

© Oxford University Press. Permission granted to reproduce for classroom use.

Part 1

Write one or two words to complete each activity. If a word is not needed, write an X. Then match each activity to its meaning.

1. _____ own place
2. _____ weight
3. _____ of debt
4. _____ of my parents' home
5. _____ money better
6. _____ better shape
7. _____ financially independent
8. _____ graduate school
9. _____ be more confident

A. to pay all your bills so you don't owe money to anyone

B. stop living with mom and dad

C. use money more carefully

D. start living in your own apartment

E. do more exercising and be healthier

F. have enough money so I can pay all my bills on my own

G. weigh less than I do now

H. study for an advanced degree at a university after finishing a first degree

I. believe more strongly that I can do something

Part 2

Which goals in Part 1 do you have now? Choose the six most important goals. Put them in order from the one you can achieve the soonest to the one that will take the longest. In class, talk about your ideas with a partner.

_____   _____

_____   _____

_____   _____

Part 3

Complete the conversations with your own goals and wishes. In class, practice the conversations with a partner.

1.

Meg: What would you like to do by the end of this English course?

You: _____.

2.

Sharon: What do you wish you could do?

You: _____.

Lesson 32   **73**

Vocabulary Worksheet Answer Keys

Vocabulary Worksheet 1

Part 1
1. B 4. H 7. C
2. F 5. G 8. A
3. D 6. E

Part 2
1. an only child 3. single, spouse
2. engaged 4. firstborn

Vocabulary Worksheet 2

Part 1
Answers will vary. Sample answer.
Positive: a role model, an optimist, a born leader, a problem solver
Negative: a loner, a pessimist, a know-it-all
Both: a follower

Part 2
Answers will vary. Sample answer.
1. A president
2. role model, an optimist
3. problem solver
4. know-it-alls
5. My dad, my mom
6. be careful about what he/she says
7. sees how to make a situation better
8. Ruth, born leader
9. shy

Vocabulary Worksheet 3

Part 1
1. moody 5. flexible
2. reliable 6. immature
3. considerate 7. forgiving
4. mature 8. responsible

Part 2
Alternative answers provided in parentheses.
1. reliable 5. moody
2. mature 6. immature
3. flexible 7. responsible (reliable)
4. forgiving 8. considerate

Part 3
1. responsible 4. flexible
2. mature 5. considerate
3. forgiving 6. reliable
B: So your sister needs to be more reliable.

Vocabulary Worksheet 4

Alternative answers provided in parentheses.
1. friendship (compassion, kindness)
2. loyalty (kindness)
3. respect
4. honesty
5. sacrifice (kindness)
6. courage, compassion (kindness, friendship, sacrifice)
7. determination
8. compassion (kindness, sacrifice)
9. sportsmanship, kindness

Vocabulary Worksheet 5

Part 1
Answers will vary. Sample answer.
1. d convenient location, meet new people
2. a comfortable, room service
3. b many TV channels, some have swimming pools
4. e nature, campfires
5. c eat meals together, meet people from around the world

Part 2
Answers will vary. Sample answer.
Business center: youth hostel
Pool: motel
Both: hotel
Neither: dorm, campground

Part 3
Answers will vary. Sample answer.
1. I prefer to stay in a double because there is more room.
2. I think it's better to make a reservation. You can get the room for less money.

Vocabulary Worksheet 6

Part 1
1. E 6. G
2. J 7. B
3. A 8. F
4. H 9. C
5. I 10. D

Part 2
Answers will vary. Sample answer.
2. You can keep your key. You don't have to give it to the front desk when you leave.
3. Please keep the noise to a minimum.
4. You're not allowed to swim in the pool between 10 p.m. and 8 a.m.

5. Guests are not permitted to park in front of the hotel. Please talk to the front desk if you need to park your car.
6. Please use the bathroom fan when taking a shower.
7. You can use the health club 24 hours a day.
8. Keep your valuables in the safe. We are not responsible for loss.
9. Only club members are allowed to use the lounge on the 25th floor.
10. You can order tea and coffee with room service.

Vocabulary Worksheet 7

Part 1
Answers will vary. Sample answer.
Students' additions in bold.
Campground: **campfire area**
Campground and Youth hostel: **washing machine**
Youth hostel: **lockers**
Youth hostel and Hotel: bed, lamp, **convenience store in lobby**
Hotel: TV, desk, closet, **MP3 dock**
Hotel and Campground: **restaurant**
All three: shower, sink, toilet, **parking area**

Part 2
Answers will vary. Sample answer.
1. The remote control isn't working at all.
2. The pillows are very dirty.
3. The toilet is leaking.
4. The carpet is very dirty.

Vocabulary Worksheet 8

Part 1
Answers will vary. Sample answer.
8 a restaurant server
6 a train reservations agent
1 a flight attendant
2 a travel agent
4 a salesclerk
3 a hotel clerk
7 a bus driver
5 a parking attendant

Part 2
2. I I'd
3. Do Would (or like want)
4. Would Do (or want like)
5. No Yes
6. appreciating appreciate

Part 3

1. a bus driver
2. a salesclerk
3. a restaurant server
4. a travel agent
5. a flight attendant
6. a hotel clerk

Vocabulary Worksheet 9

Part 1

Answers will vary. Sample answer.
More than once a month: food court
Once a month: boutique, hair salon, travel agency
Few times a year/Never: health food store, dry cleaners, electronics store, office supply store

Part 2

Answers will vary. Sample answer.
1. I'd go to the food court in the mall. It's got food from all over the world.
2. A haircut is about $30.
3. Sorry, I have no idea.
4. Yes, there's a section on the second floor of the grocery store over there.
5. Sorry, there isn't. The nearest one is across from the main train station.

Vocabulary Worksheet 10

Across
1. undercharged
3. change
5. misspelled
6. missing
Down
2. receipt
4. overcharged

Vocabulary Worksheet 11

Part 1

1. veterinarian
2. hair stylist
3. wedding planner
4. career counselor
5. academic adviser
6. photographer
7. computer technician
8. doctor

Vocabulary Worksheet 12

Part 1

Alternative answers are provided in parentheses.
1. I'm forgetful.
2. I'm broke.
3. I'm overwhelmed. (I'm stressed.)
4. I'm stressed.
5. I'm sleepy.
6. I'm depressed.
7. I'm lonely.
8. I'm sick.

Part 2

Answers will vary. Sample answer.
1. A: One thing you should do is go to bed earlier.
   B: I don't really like that idea. It's hard for me to sleep, even if I go to bed early.
Problem: I'm sleepy.
2. A: You could go to the doctor.
   B: That's a good idea.
Problem: I'm sick.
3. A: Something else you could do is eat out less often. You'd save a lot of money.
   B: I'm not so sure about that. It's expensive to cook for one person, and it takes time.
Problem: I'm broke.
4. A: You should use some tricks to remember things.
   B: I hadn't thought of that.
Problem: I'm forgetful.
5. A: You could make a list with the most important things you have to do at the top.
   B: I like that idea.
Problem: I'm stressed. / I'm overwhelmed.

Vocabulary Worksheet 13

Part 1

Students should circle:
playground, bully, checkers, hopscotch, zoo, tomboy

Part 2

What do you remember about your childhood?
Answers to the question will vary.
Sample answer.
I remember swimming during summer vacations. It was really great!

Vocabulary Worksheet 14

Part 1

Answers will vary. Sample answer.
Positive: lucky, romantic
Negative: awful, embarrassing, scary, disgusting
Both: strange

Part 2

1. ~~says~~ said
2. ~~What~~ How
3. ~~hasn't~~ hadn't
4. ~~will~~ would
5. ~~told to~~ told
6. ~~love~~ loved

Vocabulary Worksheet 15

Part 1

1. cancels
2. donates
3. saves
4. catches
5. breaks
6. closes
7. causes
8. crashes
9. denies
10. scores

Part 2

2. touch
3. allow
4. fix
5. accept
6. change
7. miss
8. take
9. find

Part 3

Answers will vary. Sample answer.
1. Yes. I've donated clothes and money.
2. cars, bikes, planes

Vocabulary Worksheet 16

Part 1

1. a natural disaster   earthquakes
3. a political change   elections
4. a sporting success   winning gold in the Olympics
2. a key discovery   cure for cancer
7. a royal wedding   Diana and Charles
6. a celebrity scandal   Tiger Woods
5. a daring rescue   bus driver saves children on burning bus

Part 2

Answers will vary. Sample answer.
1. When were the last
   2012
2. When did Prince William and Catherine Middleton get married?
   royal, April, 2011
3. When did London host the Olympics?
   London, the Olympics, 2012
4. When was U.S. President Barack Obama elected?
   Obama, on November, 2008
5. When did Wen Jiabao become the Premier of China
   He, the Premier, 2003

Vocabulary Worksheet 17

Part 1

Answers will vary. Sample answer.
Weather: an acquaintance
Weather and Personal problems:
Personal problems: a childhood friend
Personal problems and Fun things to do: a best friend
Fun things to do and Weather: a fair-weather friend
Fun things to do: an old friend
All three: a lifelong friend
Don't talk about any: a former friend

Part 2

Answers will vary. Sample answer.
1. A: hasn't called me for a few days
   B: He hasn't?
2. A: we talked for hours
   B: You did?
3. A: Rob, we don't see each other very often
   B: You don't?

Vocabulary Worksheet 18

Part 1
Answers will vary. Sample answer.

4 accepting   g
1 reliable   a
5 forgiving   d
2 truthful   b
6 loyal   c
3 supportive   e
7 caring   f

Part 2
Answers will vary. Sample answer.

1. reliable
2. truthful
3. supportive
4. I do, but not as important as some other things.
5. a colleague needs to be truthful
6. reliable, truthful.
7. being loyal is important, too
8. supportive
9. a boss needs to be forgiving, too

Vocabulary Worksheet 19

Part 1
Answers will vary. Sample answer.

4 take a class   Sounds fun.
3 join a student club   It could be fun. What club?
1 make friends through friends   We probably like the same things.
9 introduce yourself to people   I'm shy.
5 join an online group   I can't type very quickly.
8 go to social events   I wouldn't know what to talk about.
6 use social networks   I want to meet people, not just online.
7 play sports   What if I'm bad at the sport?
2 do volunteer work   I could help people and meet new people at the same time. Sounds great!

Part 2
Answers will vary. Sample answer.

1. make friends through friends
2. Yeah, because we probably like the same things.
3. I wouldn't feel comfortable doing that.
4. to do volunteer work
5. you can help people and meet new people at the same time
6. That sounds like it could be fun.
7. I wouldn't feel comfortable doing volunteer work.
8. We should join an online group

Vocabulary Worksheet 20

Part 1
1. feelings
2. ignored
3. apologize
4. problems
5. involve
6. joke

Part 2
1. problems
2. ignored
3. joke
4. apologize
5. feelings
6. involve

Part 3
Answers will vary. Sample answer.

1. my sister's birthday last month
2. my history test last week, on my desk
3. I hadn't borrowed money from my friend. It's been a problem ever since then.

Vocabulary Worksheet 21

Part 1
Answers will vary. Sample answer.
For free: leadership, computer skills, work experience, knowledge of current affairs
Takes money: overseas experience, a graduate degree
For free, and Takes money (middle of diagram): communication skills, good school grades, fluency in English

Part 2
Answers may vary. Sample answer.
Have now: computer skills
Want/want more of: fluency in English, overseas experience

Vocabulary Worksheet 22

Part 1
Answers will vary. Sample answer.

1 fast food
3 online travel service   lowest prices, flexible travel
2 soft drinks   no calories, famous people drink them
5 office supplies   helps us work, low cost
6 bus line   convenience, no parking problems
4 amusement park   experience another world, have fun
7 hair coloring   look younger, change your image

Part 2
Answers will vary. Sample answer.
Something necessary: office supplies, bus line
Something fun: hair coloring, amusement park, soft drinks
Something fun and Something necessary: sportswear, fast food

Vocabulary Worksheet 23

Part 1
1. language school
2. airline
3. supermarket
4. convenience store
5. shopping mall
6. bank

Part 2
Answers will vary. Sample answer.
Banks are becoming popular on the Internet.
None of them can be completely replaced by the Internet because shopping is a hobby and something some people enjoy doing.

Part 3
Answers will vary. Sample answer.

1. I rarely go to shopping malls because I don't like shopping.
2. Yes, I do.
3. I go to convenience stores almost every day.
4. Yes, I have.
5. The nearest supermarket is just down the street.
6. I can buy laundry soap, uncooked meat, and brooms at a supermarket.
7. *Skyways* is the most popular airline in my country.

Vocabulary Worksheet 24

Part 1
Answers will vary. Sample answer.

2 location   1 idea
4 marketing   3 prices
6 logo   5 service

Part 2
Answers will vary. Sample answer.

1. logo
2. location
3. marketing
4. prices
5. idea
6. service

Vocabulary Worksheet 25

Part 1
1. decline
2. bow
3. acknowledge
4. shake
5. pour
6. accept
7. expected

Part 2
Answers will vary. Sample answer.

1. It's impolite to stand your chopsticks in a bowl of rice.
2. You're expected to bow when you meet others.
3. You're expected to show respect to older people when you say hello.
4. You're supposed to pour drinks for others.
5. At parties, it's not the custom to pour drinks for yourself.

6. It's the custom to take off your shoes before you enter someone's home.
7. It's polite to take a small gift when visiting someone.
8. It's the custom to exchange business cards when meeting for the first time.
9. You're supposed to say, "Leave and come back" when you leave in the morning.
10. You're expected to show respect to teachers.
11. It's impolite to take potted plants when you visit someone in the hospital.
12. It's polite to use formal language when talking to teachers.

Part 3

Answers will vary. Sample answer.
Twice.
Ten times.

Vocabulary Worksheet 26

Across
2. virtue   6. ignorance
Down
1. haste   4. charity
2. variety   5. knowledge
3. diligence
Answers will vary. Sample answer.
Across
2. Good character
6. Not having knowledge or education
Down
1. Making decisions or acting too quickly
2. Many kinds
3. Being careful and working hard
4. Giving money, food, and other things to people who are poor or need help
5. Information. Understanding. Skill from experience.

Vocabulary Worksheet 27

Part 1

Students should circle:
mirror, ladder, coin, umbrella, calendar, shadow

Part 2

You'll have bad luck if you see a white cat at night.
No, I don't agree, because I don't think cats are lucky or unlucky.

Vocabulary Worksheet 28

Part 1

Across
2. costume   7. aliens
4. reflection   9. ghost
5. bear   10. fake
6. gorilla

Down
1. aircraft   5. balloon
2. creature   8. smoke
3. UFO

Part 2

Answers will vary. Sample answer.
Across
2. Something a person wears to look like someone or something else.
4. Something you see in a mirror, lake, etc.
5. A big animal that can hurt people. It's often in the woods.
6. A very large ape or monkey.
7. People or things from outer space.
9. Something that seems like a person's spirit after he/she dies.
10. Not real.
Down
1. Anything that can fly in the air.
2. Any kind of animal.
3. A ship from outer space.
5. Something that gets bigger when air is put in it.
8. The gray or white thing that is made when we burn something.

Vocabulary Worksheet 29

Part 1

Answers will vary. Sample answer.
All the time: language teachers, cash, printed books
Sometimes: landline phones, laptops, credit cards, watches
Never: gas-powered cars, DVDs

Part 2

1. ~~all~~ most   4. ~~would~~ will
2. ~~may~~ will   5. ~~may~~ will (OR delete probably)
3. ~~like~~ likely   6. ~~would~~ will

Part 3

1. P   4. D
2. D   5. P
3. D   6. D

Vocabulary Worksheet 30

Part 1

1. ice caps   a   5. fresh water   b
2. animal   h   6. storms   c
   species
3. cities   e   7. sea levels   d
4. rainforests   f   8. coral reefs   g

Part 2

Answers will vary. Sample answer.
Oceans: coral reefs
Oceans and Land: ice caps, sea levels, animal species
Land: storms, rainforests, fresh water, cities

Vocabulary Worksheet 31

Part 1

Answers for chores will vary. Sample answer. Additional answers provided in parentheses, but the meanings are different than those studied.
1. up (out)
2. out (up, away, off)   the refrigerator, the cabinet
3. out (away, up, off)   the trash, the old magazines
4. away (out, off)   the clothes, the laundry
5. out (off, up)   the trash, the bottles
6. off (away, up, out)   the table, the desk
7. off (out)   the children, my sister
8. up (out)   my coat, the calendar

Part 2

Answers will vary. Sample answer.
Every day: wipe off the table, put away the laundry, hang up my coat
Several times a week: throw out the old magazines, pick up the room, clean out the cabinet
Never: take out the trash, drop off my sister

Part 3

Answers will vary. Sample answer.
1. take out the trash
2. clean out the cabinets
3. wipe off the table

Vocabulary Worksheet 32

Part 1

1. get my   D
2. lose   G
3. get out   A
4. move out   B
5. manage   C
6. get in   E
7. be   F
8. go to   H
9. X   I

Part 2

Answers will vary. Sample answer.
move out of my parents' home
get my own place
manage money better
get in better shape
lose weight
go to graduate school

Part 3

Answers will vary. Sample answer.
1. I'd like to be more fluent in English.
2. I wish I could be financially independent.

Confidence Booster Answer Keys

- Instead of having students always be A or B, have them switch for every other Confidence Booster. This will allow them to take turns starting the conversations in Part 2.

- If some pairs finish quickly, have them personalize the material while waiting. For example, for Confidence Booster 5-8, have them make their own rules for student dorms or another setting (for example, the English classroom).

- To challenge students, have them create one or more conversations using some or all of the responses they didn't use in Part 2.

Answers

- Answers for Part 1 can be found by comparing Student A and Student B pages in the Student Book.

Pages 82 and 90
1–4   Do you need to be loyal?

2
2. a   **3.** a   **4.** b   **5.** a   **6.** a   **7.** b

Pages 83 and 91
5–8   What is the rule?

2
2. a   **3.** b   **4.** a   **5.** a   **6.** b   **7.** b

Pages 84 and 92
9–12   What is the reason?

2
2. a   **3.** b   **4.** b   **5.** a   **6.** a   **7.** a

Pages 85 and 93
13–16   Nick used to play checkers.

2
2. b   **3.** b   **4.** b   **5.** a   **6.** b   **7.** a

Pages 86 and 94
17–20   How does she know him?

2
2. b   **3.** b   **4.** a   **5.** a   **6.** a   **7.** a

Pages 87 and 95
21–24   What is the job?

2
2. b   **3.** a   **4.** b   **5.** a

Pages 88 and 96
25–28   How can we succeed?

2
2. b   **3.** a   **4.** a   **5.** a   **6.** b   **7.** b

Pages 89 and 97
29–32   What will you do?

2
2. b   **3.** a   **4.** a   **5.** b